THE POWER OF CHARISM

The Power of Charismatic Healing

A Personal Account

ANDY O'NEILL

THE MERCIER PRESS LTD.
FOWLER WRIGHT BOOKS LTD.

The Mercier Press Limited
4 Bridge Street, Cork
24 Lower Abbey Street, Dublin 1

© Andy O'Neill, 1985

British Library Cataloguing in Publication Data

O'Neill, Andy
  The power of charismatic healing.
  1. Pastoral medicine   2. Pastoral psychology
  I. Title
  265'.82   BV4337

Reprinted 1985

The Mercier Press Ltd. ISBN 0 85342 749 6
Fowler Wright Books Ltd. ISBN 0 85244 038 3

Printed by Litho Press Co., Midleton, Co. Cork.

Contents   •

To my sister Maureen, through whom it all began, to my friends Joe FitzPatrick and Colm Scalon who for years have pestered me to write it all down and to my wife Delia with love and gratitude.

1

Personal Experience

On an August evening in 1976 I received a telephone call to my Blackrock home. It was my sister Maureen calling from Waterford. She informed me that she was coming to Dublin for a weekend to attend a conference and, indicating the date, wished to know could she stay with me. She explained that she would be engaged at the conference on the Friday night and all day on Saturday and Sunday. So her visit to me would only be on a bed and breakfast basis. After a quick check with my wife Delia, I told her she would be welcome at our house and arranged to pick her up outside the Royal Dublin Society, Dublin, when the first session of the conference ended on the Friday night. I put down the telephone and did not think this affair would be of any consequence, other than a normal visit from a member of my family. What I did not know was that this seemingly simple visit of my sister was to be the beginning of a series of events which would radically and totally change my life and dramatically affect the lives of many people.

On the Friday night as arranged, I drove to the Royal Dublin Society conference hall, arriving at approximately 10.30 pm, and was surprised to find cars parked literally everywhere. Buses were queued up and thousands of people were pouring out of the exits, men, women, boys, girls, brothers, priests, regular and secular, and nuns galore. I mingled with them, endeavouring to spot my sister. These people looked and sounded joyfully animated, and were chatting away excitedly. There were hugs, kisses, and handshakes all round me. It reminded me of a scene outside a sports stadium after a big match, with one extraordinary difference – there seemed to be no losers.

I eventually found my sister in the crowd, extracted her from an excited group, put her in my car and headed home. Her first words were, 'Andy, what a wonderful night I have had!' She seemed to be aglow. For me it was just another Friday night, the end of the usual stressful working week and hopefully the eve of two days of freedom and relaxation after the tension and strain of the business world. Driving home through the heavy city traffic, my sister chatted away about the conference. It was she informed me, the Irish National Conference of the Charismatic Movement. Her chat mostly passed over my head, as I kept my eyes on the road. All I wanted was to get home to bed and was looking forward to waking up the following morning to experience the glorious feeling of not having to go to work. But then I soon realised that there could be no 'lie in' for me, as my sister told me, she had an appointment to meet her friends outside the conference hall at 8.00 am on the Saturday morning. So I concluded that the sooner I got to bed, the better. After the customary cup of tea and a chat with my wife, we set the alarm clock for 6.30 am, and I hit the sack, very tired.

On Saturday I found myself driving my sister along the Merrion Road, at the ridiculous hour of 7.45 am. Many people were already walking towards the conference venue. We picked up a pair of nuns who were delighted to get the lift and they chatted away merrily to my sister. The good sisters asked was I enjoying the conference and just for fun I told them that I couldn't understand all this fuss about religion, being an atheist myself! They laughed that one off, but I was very sure in my own mind that there was a hundred and one other things I would rather do than spend a whole Saturday at that conference. Stopping outside the entrance to the hall, I was surprised to see a queue of people already formed and cars beginning to arrive. I dropped my passengers, headed home, and dismissed the whole affair from my mind.

While working in the garden on Saturday afternoon and listening to sport on BBC Radio 2, I thought of my sister's involvement in this charismatic renewal affair and remembered her telling me from time to time of a prayer meeting she attended in her home town, Waterford. But I had always concluded that such a scene was not for me. Attendance at prayer meetings would not fit in with my life style. Then suddenly for no reason at all, I found myself reviewing my life. I was an action man. I was Area Manager for an insurance company in Dublin and worked hard in this highly competitive and stressful profession, never counting the hours. I was in the results business. I liked the odd game of golf and swimming – in warm weather! I suppose I could also be described as a middle of the road Catholic with a life long membership of the Society of St Vincent de Paul. My Vincentian activity at this particular time was visiting patients in St Vincent's Hospital close to my home. So cutting the grass in the garden and enjoying the sunshine, I ended this quick review of my life, concluding that I had nothing in common with these people down the road from me at the Royal Dublin Society that weekend. Just at that moment I was doing what I wanted to be doing, where I wanted to be doing it and in no way did I wish to be disturbed. Anyway on the radio the news was that Arsenal had scored a second goal! Then suddenly my daughter Hilary appeared and said, 'Oh, Dad, would you ever drive me to Dunnes' Stores. I need a pair of tights.' I hesitated for just a moment, wondering whether or not to swap the gentle garden scene for the urgent noise of traffic on a major road. But once more accepting that fathers can't win, I switched off the radio, left the haven of the garden and drove my daughter the two miles or so to the supermarket at Cornelscourt, slightly huffed that my afternoon had been disturbed.

Arriving at the supermarket car park, I stayed in the car, informing Hilary that I would wait for her there. Exactly opposite where I had parked I noticed what appeared to be a small temporary chapel. I left the car and decided to visit it. I went in and found Mass in progress. About twenty people were there. I knelt down but was immediately struck by a very strange atmosphere. There was an extraordinary silence there. Nobody seemed to move about or even cough and strangely several small children there made no noise at all. A bearded priest whispered the Mass. The little hut in that crowded busy supermarket car park seemed totally cut off from the bustling world outside. There, I was conscious of a sensation which I had never previously experienced but which somehow reminded me of the effect the crowds had on me as they streamed out of the Royal Dublin Society the previous night. This sensation was something which I could not understand, identify or define. The priest distributed Holy Communion, finished Mass and was gone. The little congregation dispersed and a young man in his late teens and myself were the only ones left. I turned to him perplexed, and asked, 'What was so different about that Mass and that priest?'

'Hasn't he an extraordinary charismatic presence?' he simply replied.

I couldn't comprehend this remark, slowly left the chapel, and returned to the car, confused.

In a few minutes my daughter Hilary appeared. I was sitting in the car when she left and was in the same position when she returned. She had no idea that I had ever left the car. But immediately she sensed something. 'Dad,' she said, 'what's happened – your face has changed?'

'I don't know, Hilary, but I have just encountered something extraordinary,' I replied. I drove on in silence but my daughter insisted on knowing what happened. So I told her of my visit to the little chapel, where I had an experience which, while very real, baffled me, and which I was quite unable to describe or explain. Hilary made no reply but this sensation or experience, whatever it was, remained with me for the rest of the day.

The conference ended for my sister on the Sunday night and in our house after an evening meal, describing the events of her weekend, asked would we like to hear three or four thousand people singing in tongues. She had taped it at the conference. Being totally ignorant of this tongues business, I said, 'Well that's real mental hospital stuff, but play it anyway and I'll tell you what I think of it.' She did so and once again I was shocked and puzzled, as I wondered what was happening to me. The tape ran for about a minute or two but I insisted on her playing it again and again. I must have sounded like the 'Play it again, Sam' character. I'm sure I listened to it half a dozen times. My sister asked, 'What are you getting from it, Andy?'

'I don't know, Maureen, but it sounds like a choir, or an organ, or an orchestra, or a peal of joy bells, or maybe a combination of all of them,' I replied. I now wanted to know about these tongues, how it starts and stops in a prayer meeting. My sister answered as best she could, adding, 'Why don't you go to a prayer meeting and experience it for yourself?'

'It is all right for you – you attend one in Waterford but where would I find one of these meetings in Dublin?' I said.

'There is one in St Augustine's every Tuesday night,' she answered.

St Augustine's is a St John of God foundation opposite the house where I live! What a weekend I was having! My sister continued, 'Please, Andy, go and see it. I believe,' she went on, 'that the Charismatic Renewal Movement is the manifestation of the power of the Holy Spirit in our age, and what is more, I am certain it is tailor-made for you.'

I went to sleep on that night thinking of all the unusual things which had happened to me during the weekend – the strange sensation I experienced mixing with the crowds on the Friday night, which was repeated on the Saturday afternoon in the tiny chapel in a supermarket car park and yet again in my home listening to a tape on the Sunday night.

The following Tuesday evening, on my way home from visiting the sick in St Vincent's Hospital, I saw people streaming into the grounds of St Augustine's and wondered would these people be going to a prayer meeting. I parked the car and decided to follow them. Walking through the grounds of that monastery , I suddenly became very uncertain and confused, asking myself what was I doing there and why I needed this thing. After all, I reasoned, one can't join every organisation which comes along. Anyway, I assured myself, I was quite all right without this prayer meeting business. I continued to reason with myself, realising that there were, thankfully no great moral problems in my life. I was happily married, totally involved in my job, and a member of the Society of St Vincent de Paul. Why get entangled in this prayer movement, I asked myself? However I decided to go in and have a look accepting that at least I could then telephone my sister and tell her that I was at one of her strange gatherings. I entered a hallway, saw a young man standing at a door, and enquired as to the whereabouts of the prayer meeting. 'You are in the right spot, but there is a period of silence being observed at the moment,' he replied quietly.

After a few moments he ushered me into the hall and led me to a chair. I saw about one hundred and fifty to two hundred people. But straightaway I remember making a quick decision. Being in management in business, decision-making was nothing new to me. I promised myself that I was not going to be fooled by anything or anybody. Whatever was going on in that hall I was not going to participate. I decided to just sit there and take a cool clinical scientific look at it, making sure not to become involved in any way.

Strangely once more I was surprised, as after a few minutes in that hall, the same sensation which I had experienced on the Friday, Saturday and Sunday of the previous weekend, was again with me. I looked around and listened and for the first time in my life, at that prayer meeting, I saw and heard people specifically, openly, out loud, unashamedly and together, praising God. I immediately began comparing what I was hearing to my way of praying. I then realised that my prayers were strictly confined to 'gimmie prayers' – 'Lord, give me'. . . 'Lord I want'. . . 'for myself'. . . 'for my wife'. . . 'for my family'. . . 'for my career'. . . 'for my business'. . .

Astonishingly, it also appeared that these people, whom I was looking at and listening to, had a new freedom of prayer which I never even knew existed. If I didn't like or approve of what they were doing, then that was just too bad. They were doing their own thing and doing it, apparently, joyfully. If they felt like raising their voices in praise of God, they did so. In songs of praise to the Lord, well if they felt like lifting their arms and clapping their hands, they did just that. At that precise moment and possibly because I was in the presence of so many joyful people and conscious that there was no joy in me at all, the old saying came to me, 'To hell with the begrudgers!' I was shocked to think that it might apply to me.

Next I heard the tongues for the first time, in the flesh. I thought that a sane and sensible chap like myself would be embarrassed or turned off hearing people express themselves in this way, but I wasn't. I found the singing in tongues somehow consoling and the silence which followed seemed to bring great peace to the faces of the people there. The prayer meeting seemed to have many twists and turns. Next I heard people reading Scripture aloud and immediately realised that the last time I read Scripture was at school – when I had to! But these people appeared to be very familiar with Scripture. Then others stood up and witnessed what the Lord was doing in their lives. The newness of it all plus the joyful guitar music seemed to bowl me over. The whole scene was totally different from any religious gathering that I had ever previously witnessed and then out of the blue I may have had a road to Damascus Pauline experience. Suddenly, my whole life seemed to appear before me, on a chart as it were, with a line drawn down the centre. On the left hand side of that line I saw all the things which would have to go out of my life, should I want to meet the Lord in this new way. There was nothing greatly out of control in my life, I knew, but somehow the world and all its trappings, which I sought constantly and loved, would in some way have to take second place, should I want to be part of this extraordinary challenging and attractive way of life which appeared to be opening up before me. Strangely, I can't remember seeing anything at all on the right hand side of that imaginary chart!

The prayer meeting ended and I went home puzzled, confused, quiet, but surprisingly very very curious.

2

'A Funny Way to Spend
Tuesday Nights'

For the next few weeks I was drawn back to that prayer meeting every Tuesday night and was startled to find as the weeks went by, that the promise of non-involvement which I had made to myself at the first encounter with a charismatic renewal meeting, was fading away, if not gone completely. The absolute necessity to look at the prayer meeting with a cool clinical scientific attitude now seemed no longer urgent. Within three months I was at the stage when I looked forward to Tuesday nights, knowing that I could go to that prayer meeting, sit down comfortably, close my eyes should I feel like it, and push aside business and family cares and worries, at least for a few hours, while listening to people singing the praises of the Lord. I remember being very shocked when I realised that outside that prayer meeting there was virtually no relaxation in my life style at any other level.

Some months after my first exposure to charismatic renewal, I attended a weekend national Conference of the Society of St Vincent de Paul which was held at St Patrick's Training College, Dublin. On the Saturday night of this conference, an impromptu concert was organised. It quickly developed into a sing-song, with a few drinks for the people who needed them. At this concert I met Fr Frank Maher, a Vincentian priest who was there with his music group of young people, all involved in the Charismatic Renewal Movement, who were present to lead a short optional prayer session prior to the concert. We chatted away in this large, noisy hall while I told this group of my first reactions to my recent exposure to a prayer meeting. Frank Maher suddenly began quizzing me concerning my commitment to Vincentian work and my general life style. He withdrew his chair from the group and closed his eyes for a few moments. Then he quickly rejoined us saying, 'Boys and girls, I have just had a word from the Lord that we are to baptise Andy in the Holy Spirit right here and now.' His announcement was greeted with enthusiastic cheers and immediately in that smoke filled hall where hundreds of people were singing and chatting, I found myself surrounded by Frank Maher and his music group, who laid their hands on me, while praying and singing in tongues. Being totally ignorant of the philosophy or theology of this Baptism in the Holy Spirit business, I just hadn't a clue as to what was going on. This time I had no sensations or experiences and was completely unmoved. The whole incident took about ten minutes and despite some strange and puzzling looks from people clustered at nearby tables, the group gathered around me carried on regardless.

They informed me that the job was done and Frank Maher and his boys and girls hugged and congratulated me. I had no idea what the fuss was all about and driving home that night, dismissed the whole incident from my mind.

But all the time the tongues fascinated me. I assumed that it was not for me and when the Lord was being praised in that manner at prayer meetings, I prayed in my own way, using short phrases such as 'Praise the Lord' and 'Praise God', but ever so quietly, in case anyone should hear me. Next I began repeating snatches of the old Latin Mass, for no apparent reason, while the tongues was in progress. Then on the night of the prayer meeting immediately following my Baptism in the Spirit, sitting on a chair, totally relaxed, with my eyes closed, I suddenly heard myself uttering strange sounds, which simply flowed from me, effortlessly. These sounds seemed like a mixture of the Romance languages, reminding me of blurred French, Latin, Spanish or Italian words and were both musical and soft. At the end of the prayer meeting, people sitting near me confirmed that I had received the gift of tongues. But at that stage I was totally ignorant of the meaning and function of this phenomenon.

Some weeks after receiving the gift of tongues, I attended the weekly prayer meeting at which there was a teaching on one of the gifts of the Holy Spirit, the gift of healing. I was more than a little interested because as I've already said I visited patients in St Vincent's Hospital once a week. I visited them solely in the belief that such visits would be acknowledged by the Lord as done to himself. But there the religious philosophy content of my visits ended, as I had never prayed with patients, spoke of the Lord to them, nor did I ever intend to do so. Actually I felt that should I be sick in hospital and should some 'Holy Joe' approach to speak religion to me, I would tell him very quickly to scram and would be very tempted to add, 'You're all right, Jack, in your health and strength – it is easy for you to pray!'

But here at this prayer meeting, the man giving the teaching appeared to be challenging me, saying, 'The Lord has the power to heal. When you are in the presence of sickness, would you ever have the faith – and it takes more courage than faith – to lay your hands on a sick person and say in the name of Jesus Christ be healed!' There I was, boy and man, Catholic all my life and now for the first time ever I was hearing of the laying on of hands, in the name of the Lord, to heal the sick. Up to that point in time in my life, I had never before heard of this Christian way of healing. Neither priest, brother, nun, missioner or anybody of such commitment, had ever advocated it, to my knowledge. Somehow the challenge of that teaching stayed with me but I never even contemplated doing anything about it. However two strange events were about to catch up with me.

As I was leaving the Tuesday night prayer meeting some weeks after the teaching on healing, a man approached me. He asked, 'Andy, will you pray with me?'

I was astonished. In the past, I mused, I must have received thousands of invitations to do things and to go places, but now for the first time ever, here was a man inviting me to pray with him!

'What is your Christian name?' I asked.

'Michael,' he replied.

Then I asked what his problem was, as if I had a right to know!

'Andy, with the stress and strain of running my own business, plus the worry of a seriously ill wife, as I speak to you now I am as rigid as an iron bar,' he replied.

So I put my hands on his shoulders and asked him to do likewise to me. This was the first time I had ever touched a human being in prayer and immediately I received what I now know to be the gift of spontaneous prayer. I said something like, 'Lord, bless Michael. Come into his work situation, and whether he is buying or selling, manufacturing, wholesaling, retailing or servicing, bless his undertaking. Bless his customers, staff, directors, the tax men, the vat man, his accountants and his bank manager. Bless everyone who touches his business in any way, and take all the tension from Michael. And Lord, please also accept my hands on Michael as being on his sick wife, as they are two in the one flesh, and heal her, Lord.'

Then for the first time ever I prayed from Scripture, reminding both myself and Michael of the way the Lord takes care of the lilies of the field, who do no work at all but who are so beautifully arrayed by him. But at the words of Scripture 'Why are you fearful, you of little faith', a remarkable thing happened – my hands on Michael's shoulders dropped, I am sure, two to three inches. His shoulders had been hunched up. He didn't realise this nor was I conscious of it when he came to me. But down his shoulders came suddenly and together. I don't know which of us got the greater shock! 'Michael, what's happened?' I exclaimed.

'I don't know, Andy, but I am totally relaxed!' he replied.

With that, he hugged me, his face transformed with a huge grin. He left me with a spring in his step. I walked very slowly out to my car and went home.

The following Tuesday night after the prayer meeting, Michael came to me and introduced me to his wife. She appeared to be radiant and told me that while her husband was at the previous prayer meeting, she became very well and wished to thank me for the prayers. I just didn't know what to say to this very happy and relaxed couple. The first of the two strange events had caught up with me.

On the following Monday night after my experience with Michael at the prayer meeting, I went as usual to visit the sick in St Vincent's Hospital. I would normally enter one of the wards during visiting hours and seek out a patient who would be without visitors. I would then announce my name and the name of the organisation which I represented, (to take the mystery out of the visit) telling the sick person I was there for a chat, should it be acceptable. But on this particular Monday night as I entered a ward I saw a nun, a middle-aged Sister of Charity. She seemed to be a very solid, sensible person, nobody's fool (like myself!) and around life and death most of her life. On the spur of the moment I decided to chat her up concerning this Christian healing business and the laying on of hands. I thought that maybe, being a Catholic and in the medical profession, she might have some knowledge of it. I approached her and said, 'Tell me, Sister, did you ever hear of the "laying on of hands" in the name of the Lord, to heal the sick?'

'Certainly I have,' she replied. 'It was,' she continued, 'widely known and extensively used in the early Church. It has declined, but strange to say, the practice is being renewed in the Church by people in Charismatic Renewal.'

I might add, she had no idea of who I was or of my connection with Charismatic Renewal. The conversation developed as follows:

'Sister, have you ever seen this laying on of hands?' I asked.

'I haven't,' she replied.

'Would you do it?' I asked.

'I would not,' she replied.

'Why not?' I asked.

'I haven't that sort of faith,' she replied.

Then she turned the questions on me. 'Did you ever see it?'

'I think I did,' I replied, thinking of what had happened when I had my hands on Michael's shoulders.

'Would you do it?' she challenged.

'I think I would,' I replied, hesitantly.

'Very well then. I am very worried about this girl over here. Come and lay your hands on her,' she responded.

The Sister then brought me to a bed where I saw a girl whom I thought was in her late teens or early twenties. She was lying prone, motionless with her eyes closed. The Sister, who stood at one side of the bed, while I stood at the opposite side, then said, 'Off you go – lay your hands on her!'

Now I had never in my whole life seen anybody laying hands on a sick person, seeking healing in the name of the Lord. It was not in my Catholic tradition so I had neither experience of it nor training in it. I hadn't a clue as to how I should proceed. For a few moments I did nothing, but stood looking down at the motionless patient. The good Sister opposite me did not make any comment or offer any advice. So I put my hands on the patient's right forearm and said softly, 'Hello, sweetheart, Andy O'Neill is my name – would it bother you if I prayed with you?' There was no response or reaction. I didn't know whether the girl was unconscious, asleep or sedated. Suddenly I remembered some weeks previously being at a lecture on Vatican II given by a Marist priest, who said that while all prayer is acceptable to the Lord, the classical Vatican II method of prayer is the prayer to our heavenly Father, through his only begotten son Jesus Christ, by the power of the Holy Spirit. So I concluded that if such a method is advocated by Vatican II, well, who am I to argue? So leaving my hands on the patient's forearm I said very slowly and as meaningfully as I could, 'I am asking our heavenly Father, through his only begotten Son Jesus Christ, by the power of the Holy Spirit, to heal you. Praised be Jesus Christ, Amen.' Both the patient and the Sister remained motionless, but immediately the bell sounded in the ward signifying the end of the visiting hour. I just turned and fled, going through the ward door like a scalded cat. Out in the hospital corridor I remember asking myself, 'What in heaven's name is a sane and sensible chap like myself getting up to?' However, I proceeded to the teaching room in the hospital where the conference meeting of the St Vincent de Paul Society is held and promptly forgot the whole matter.

On the following Monday evening on my way to the hospital, I thought of the little girl on whom I had laid my hands and wondered was she better or worse, dead or alive, since my visit! So I decided to check it out. I entered the ward where I had found her on the previous Monday night, went to her bed, but to my surprise found the coverings rolled back as if someone had just left it. There was no sign of the patient. I turned to the lady in the next bed and enquired, 'Where is my little friend?'

'She is down in the television room,' the lady replied.

'Is she well?' I asked.

'Oh, she is very well,' she responded.

'When did she get well?' I continued.

'She became well last Monday night,' the lady answered.

'What was she suffering from?' I asked.

The lady replied that the little girl was in an epileptic coma for the previous six weeks. I was so surprised that I forgot to thank the lady, left the ward and walked to the teaching room and remained there for the best part of an hour until my colleagues assembled. I was quite unable to visit another patient that night.

At around eight o'clock one of my conference colleagues arrived and told me he had been to the television room and had chatted to a little girl, who asked him was he the person who prayed with her on the previous Monday night. He said he wasn't and there and then she told him her story. She explained that she woke out of the coma and found the Ward Sister standing over her. The Sister asked her how she was feeling and the patient replied that she felt fine. The good Sister then informed the patient that some moments previously a man had laid his hands on her and prayed for her recovery.

'Andy, was it you?' my colleague asked.

'I think it was,' I replied, very hesitantly.

My colleague, a dental surgeon, who was also a member of a charismatic renewal prayer group simply said, 'It looks as if you are in the healing ministry, old chap.'

The healing ministry? It was the first time I had heard these words.

The second strange event had arrived, so I thought it was high time for me to review my whole involvement with Charismatic Renewal, right from the start.

So looking back then, on the first few months of my exposure to Charismatic Renewal, a pattern of events seemed to have emerged and I wondered whether or not their order was of any significance. First came my sister's visit to my home and my experiences that weekend. Next followed my first attendance at a Charismatic Renewal prayer meeting and its effect on me. Then came the Baptism in the Holy Spirit in a most unlikely place and without any preparation on my part, to be followed in quick succession by the gift of tongues and two happenings which could have been healing.

At this stage I badly needed someone to talk to and sought Fr Frank Maher. Meeting him I said, 'Listen Father, since you baptised me in the Spirit I have received the gift of tongues and have apparently witnessed two healings. What's going on? Nothing like this ever happened in my life before.' He replied smilingly and seemingly with all the confidence in the world, 'Andy, this is only the beginning, only the very beginning.'

The beginning of what, I wondered? But again events coming thick and fast were to show me.

Until then, my Charismatic Renewal activity was confined to Tuesday nights at prayer meetings, with the one strange event on a Monday night in St Vincent's Hospital. But the whole scene was about to widen and change direction to encompass dramatically one of the most vital and important areas of my life.

3

'The Men in the White Coats will be Coming'

Shortly after Fr Frank Maher's 'this is only the beginning' observation I found myself in a Dublin city centre cafe, alone, around 7 pm on a Friday evening. A business client, whom I had arranged to meet there, had failed to show up – a fairly normal experience in the life of any insurance salesman. To survive in my business, one has to be an eternal optimist, so I made a note to endeavour to set up another appointment with the man concerned.

So with no further business appointments and having no commitments at home either, as my wife had a bridge date on that particular evening, I realised that I could comfortably have a night out 'on the town'. I glanced at the entertainment page on my evening newspaper but saw nothing exciting. Suddenly I remembered that the Friends Meeting House in Eustace Street was the venue for a largely attended Charismatic Renewal meeting on Friday nights. As I had never observed this scene, without more ado I headed there. It was to be one of the most important decisions of my life.

The hall was packed when I arrived and the prayer meeting progressed in the normal manner until one man stood up and addressed the meeting. He announced that he was a member of the Church of Ireland and made a point that as Christians we should ask the Lord constantly to solve every problem in our lives. Having such power at our disposal, he maintained, we were exceedingly foolish indeed not to use it. 'The Lord will do anything for you,' he continued. 'He will renew your marriage, he will cure your illness, he will heal relationships and he will protect your family, your house and your car. And if you are in business, he will even clear your desk.' At his words 'clear your desk' I sat bolt upright in my chair. I immediately thought of my very big office desk and the many hours of work I had to spend at it, day after slogging day and often into the night after office hours. The only way I could clear my desk on many occasions was by scooping everything on it into my briefcase and take it all home. Then my desk scene changed to my sitting room at night and often overflowed into the weekends. Now while I accept that I am no genius, I knew that my job efficiency was factually better than average. But for years I had completely accepted this work pattern as part of my conditions of employment. But here now was this Protestant man proclaiming that the Lord would and could clear my desk. How outrageous can these charismatics get, I mused, as I drove home after the meeting. But I was to recall vividly that Protestant man's promise during the coming week.

The Tuesday following the Eustace Street prayer meeting proved to be one of the most extraordinary days of my business career. The day progressed in the normal way but around eleven o'clock in the morning I knew exactly why I was being paid. My desk was covered with correspondence and files, each containing one more stressful problem than another. I knew that should yet another problem arrive, it and its file would have to go on the floor, as there was simply no more room on my desk. I recalled Harry Trueman's famous phrase concerning his White House desk – 'the buck stops here'. Certainly I had my share of bucks that morning. With most of the problems staring up at me I hadn't a clue as to how to solve them. I was in the classical 'business executive stress' situation, which, unfortunately, has fatal consequences for so many people in modern management. But I absolutely declined to descend into self pity as I accepted that I was in this competitive business by my own free choice, spurred on by the financial rewards. My job was to manage. Sitting stock still at my desk surveying the scene, I suddenly thought of the man's words on the previous Friday night – 'The Lord will even clear your desk!' Now one of the most fabulous men I ever met, the late Fr Tom Ahearne, always maintained that a well balanced human being should be capable of entertaining himself, entertaining his friends and entertaining a new idea. Certainly asking the Lord to clear my desk was a new idea for me. So there and then I pulled back my chair and said in my own mind, 'Lord, the longer this day goes on, the more trouble I am accumulating. Lord, the man said you would clear my desk, if I asked you. Lord, if ever I needed help, I need it now. Lord, here is my desk – You clear it for me!' I pulled my chair back to the desk, put my head down and continued with the day's work.

At one o'clock I went out to lunch and returned within the hour. Head down again, making notes, taking decisions, telephoning, dictating letters, interviewing clients and staff, setting up appointments – on and on went another day in my business life.

Then, suddenly and in some amazement, I looked at my desk. It was clear! One single solitary post card looked up at me, on which I had scribbled a telephone number and name, to ring the following day. I looked at my watch. It was 4.15 pm exactly. I was shocked, remembering the terror of the morning and then quietly reviewed the day.

Ideas and methods of solving the problems on my desk seemed to have come to me, naturally. All my telephone calls both inward and outward were totally satisfactory, letters were dictated without fuss, interviews with clients and representatives went without hassle or waffle, appointments were successfully set up – it was for me a clinically efficient and productive day. I walked into the general office and told my second-in-command that I had a call to make. I hadn't – but I couldn't think of anything else to say, I was so dumbfounded. I drove home out the Stillorgan Road so slowly that a tractor could have passed me. I wasn't in a state of shock, but I was close to it, with an empty brief case beside me on the passenger seat.

At work as a business manager I could always recognise quickly any factor which assisted or promoted my interests and would closely study it, whatever it was, to continue it and to seek to maximise it. So on that Tuesday evening at home in my sitting room with no office scene around me, I again analysed my working day, before I headed for the prayer meeting. Maybe my success was due to my dedication, experience and pure 'stickability', or it could have been due to a 'positive thinking' attitude, I reasoned. Then again it might have been all down to that old fashioned business formula – a bit of pluck and a bit of luck. But I well knew that my day radically changed when I asked the Lord to clear my desk. This was the one new factor which emerged. I concluded that I had had a very good day and so decided to repeat the formula on the following day. No manager ever changes a winning method, as Bob Paisley, one time manager of Liverpool Football Club would confirm. If the Lord had helped to clear my desk on Tuesday, I was going to afford him a similar opportunity on the

Wednesday. As a matter of fact I decided that when I would open my office door in future, I would step back and invite the Lord to enter before me. But this decision to hesitate momentarily at the office door was to bring problems – and quickly.

The three days following the 'clearing of my desk' incident were, to me, brilliant, business-wise. Not alone was my desk being cleared quickly but production was well above target. This act of standing back and letting the Lord into the office before me, was going great guns. So the next Monday morning I arrived at work as usual, full of this newly-found confidence. But pride always goes before a fall as my mother was wont to say. I opened the office door, did my special hesitation act, now for the fourth time but to my surprise, there was my senior secretary, with her chair placed well away from her desk, in a position directly in line with the door of the general office. She was sitting there looking very intently at both me and the door. She said at once, 'Mr O'Neill, what are you doing?' The surprise to me was total. There was no way I ever intended explaining this door opening routine to anybody. Seeking to gather my wits, I attempted to stall for time. 'What do you mean, Siobhán?' I replied weakly. She went straight to the point, saying, 'Mr O'Neill, you are opening that door in a very curious fashion for the last few days. As a matter of fact,' she continued, 'last Friday morning it was so noticeable that I went out into the hallway to see if there was someone with you, waiting to come in.' I was stuck to the floor. Three or four other members of the office staff put their heads up, obviously interested in developments. 'Siobhán, I am letting the Lord into the office before me,' I explained in a very weak voice. My secretary gave me a very old fashioned look and shaking her head said, 'I think, Mr O'Neill, the men in the white coats will be coming for you soon.' I was unable to comment and headed in haste to the sanctuary of my own private office. I sat down, confused, wondering whether or not this charismatic renewal business was getting out of hand. However, there was work to be done and a pile of post lay on my desk.

To begin the day I looked around for my brief case, my constant business companion, but couldn't find it. I immediately assumed that I had left it in the general office with the confusion caused by the confrontation with my secretary. I went outside but found no trace of it. Next I assumed that I had left it in my car parked nearby. I went out to the car but drew a blank there. I returned to the office and rang my wife and asked was my brief case at home. She couldn't find it either but was positive that I had left the house with it. Problems, problems. Then my wife said, 'You must have put it on the roof of the car and drove off forgetting all about it.' What a way to start a Monday morning! So it appeared that somewhere along the five miles from Blackrock to Leeson Street, one of Dublin's busiest streets, my brief case had fallen off the roof of the car. Now I had left the house shortly before eight o'clock, travelling along the Stillorgan Road, where thousands of cars travel every working morning, so one could assume that my brief case would be ripped asunder by the traffic. The only consolation in the situation was that I had never made such a mistake before and resolved never to do so again.

So on with the day's work. But this was easier said than done without my spectacles which were in my brief case and I hadn't a second pair with me. Now I use spectacles exclusively for reading and without them I can't see a hole in a ladder, print-wise. So the entire office staff knew of the lost brief case as all day long I had people reading letters for me and the notes I distributed were written in handwriting which measured nearly a quarter of an inch high.

But during the day I began to think of the people in my prayer meeting who were very deeply involved in Charismatic Renewal, their outlook and extraordinary expressions. They described themselves as people of praise and while realising that they were not better or holier than people uninvolved in the Renewal, accepted that they were different in that they constantly praised the Lord. They always insisted that tremendous power is released into any and every situation when the Lord is praised. I next wondered if praising the Lord could assist in the lost brief case affair and remembering with slight hope that my name and address was on the fly leaf of my pocket Scripture among its contents, I decided to give this method a trial. So during the day I mentally praised the Lord whenever the opportunity arose, for instance holding for a telephone call and while walking to and from lunch. But I also well knew that I had given a poor explanation to my secretary in reply to her question when I entered the office that morning.

But praising the Lord during the day had somehow restored

my confidence and as the day wore on I was convinced that my brief case would turn up against all the odds. So shortly before 5 pm I ambled into the general office and informed my secretary and any member of the office staff within earshot, that I was sure that my brief case would be returned to me, as during the day I had constantly released into the situation the power of the praising of God. My secretary looked at me but while making no verbal reply her eyes said, 'Now once a day is enough to tell a chap he is nuts, especially if he happens to be your boss.' Then it happened – the telephone rang. My secretary answered it and said, 'It is your wife, Mr O'Neill.' Taking the call in the general office I heard Delia, who was calling from home, say, 'There is a little boy here with me now and he has handed me your brief case.' He informed my wife that he found it on the Stillorgan Road while cycling to school. He opened it and saw my name and address on my Scripture. He took it to school and called with it to our house on his way home. I told Delia to give him £2 for his kindness. I thanked her and put the telephone down. My secretary and most of my office staff heard of this startling development listening to my conversation. There was total silence in the office. For the second time that day I was stuck to the floor. I remarked quietly to all and sundry, 'As these people in the Renewal tell me, there is tremendous power in the praising of God. See you all in the morning,' and I made my exit, wondering what the conversation would be like after I had left.

Driving home after witnessing strange happenings in prayer meetings, hospitals and now in my place of work, I noticed that I had no desire at all to switch on the car radio. I didn't do it on that afternoon, either. It seemed that the Lord was well and truly with me in my work situation and with the results I was experiencing, only a fool would want to change that position.

The first thing I did on my arrival home was to pick up my brief case and there plain to be seen were the marks of a car tyre on it. I opened it and took out my hard cover spectacle case, which was dented, but inside I found my spectacles, undamaged.

Into my business life, one of the most vital and important areas of my existence, on my invitation, the Lord had apparently entered with power and some style. The joy of it all continued as I listened to Delia telling me how the little boy who found my case tripped delightedly down the drive of our house, clutching his two pound notes, no doubt hoping that brief cases would continue to fall off the roofs of motor cars *ad multos annus!*

A STIFF PROPOSITION

But this pattern of strange events was to continue in my business life, with an ever widening audience. There was no witness to the clearing of my desk incident, but myself. Now all the office staff had witnessed the brief case affair. The next happening was to involve one of my outdoor representatives.

One afternoon while working in my office, my secretary informed me that James, one of my representatives wished to see me. I asked her to send him in. He entered and I rose in welcome indicating a chair to him. Noticing that he had shuffled into my office, he explained that he had developed a severe pain in his back some days previously, was unable to sit and found it difficult to walk. He appeared to be in great distress and said he was going to see his doctor that evening. So we did our business standing at my desk and I did not delay him unduly in the circumstances. As he slowly and painfully turned to leave me I wondered should I tell him about the laying on of hands experiences of mine. So I plucked up enough courage to do so and he seemed very interested. Next came the moment of truth for me and taking a deep breath I said, 'James, if you will allow me, I will lay my hands on you and ask the Lord to heal you, but should you prefer not, well that's okay by me.'

'Certainly, Mr O'Neill, what have I to lose?' he replied. Nothing, I thought to myself, except possibly the pain in your back! So I gently laid the fingers of both my hands on his back, praised the Lord and asked that the pain be taken away. He thanked me, I assisted him out of the office and helped him slide painfully into his car.

The following morning I rang James to enquire as to his condition and to hear the doctor's verdict. He answered the telephone himself and said, 'I have news for you, Mr O'Neill,' and proceeded to tell me the following story. He drove from my office to his home the previous evening and when he parked the car on his driveway, jumped out, opened the front door of his house and ran up the stairs. At the top of the stairs he stopped suddenly and only then realised that all pain, soreness and stiffness in his back had totally disappeared. 'I am about to leave for the office now,' he said and we both put down the telephones.

Shortly after that phone call, one of my secretaries, Teresa informed me that my representative, James, wished to see me but would prefer that I should come out to the general office. I did so and immediately he saw me he vaulted over the counter and then vaulted back again, saying 'How's that?' The entire office staff had seen his condition the previous afternoon and now all of them had witnessed his counter jumping act. I shook hands with him and he said, 'Thanks, so much.'

I left him, returned to my office, closed the door, sat down and did nothing for the next five minutes but I did recall Fr Frank Maher's words, 'Andy, this is only the beginning.' But out in the general office, James was busily telling the office staff of the laying on of hands business which happened in my office on the previous day. At that moment I wondered what did my staff make of the whole affair and my connection with this astonishing Charismatic Renewal Movement.

But the connection with Charismatic Renewal and my business was to continue, with yet another change of scene and personnel.

A WARM GLOW

It was late on a Friday afternoon and I was preparing to leave the office for the weekend, when I received a telephone call from a managerial colleague in Dublin. He informed me that one of our managers, from the country, was hospitalised in Dublin. My colleague was about to leave his office and visit him and asked would I like to accompany him. I agreed, and he said he would pick me up at my office within half an hour. I rang my wife, explained the new position which had arisen and we rearranged the time of our evening meal accordingly.

So at around 6 pm instead of heading home, I found myself travelling through the heavy city traffic to a hospital in the north side of Dublin. We found our colleague, who was delighted to see us, and we all enjoyed the 'crack', mostly discussing our business affairs. The patient looked seriously ill and he confided that beginning on the following Monday, his doctors had visits arranged for him to four city hospitals, all involving tests. His condition looked serious and he sounded very concerned indeed.

Coming towards the end of our visit, I wondered should I mention Charismatic Renewal to him. This was becoming quite a habit with me now when I was in the presence of sickness, I reflected. I had no contact with the patient other than meeting him at business conferences, where we exclusively talked shop and consequently I had no knowledge of his life style or outlook. However I decided to have a go and said, 'Paddy, I have been exposed to this Charismatic Renewal prayer meeting influence for some time now but it is something which you may not even have met.'

'You must be joking, Andy. There is a Charismatic Renewal prayer meeting in my house every weekend!' he replied quickly.

Would you ever know where you would be talking! So there being no need to explain things further I offered to lay my hands on him and pray for his recovery, should he wish it. He enthusiastically accepted. My colleague who had set up our visit was so embarrassed at the prospect of two grown men laying hands on each other to pray in a public hospital ward that he slowly walked away from the bed and chatted up another patient. So I laid my hands on the sick man and just then his wife arrived and I told her what we had been up to. My colleague who had wandered away, returned, re-joined us at the bedside and we made our farewells and departed.

On the following Tuesday morning I received a telephone call. It was from Paddy, my colleague in the north city hospital. Realising that I was at work, his message was short and precise. 'Andy,' he said, 'I had several tests yesterday in preparation for my attendance at other city hospitals but all the tests have been negative. I am well and I have just been discharged. The doctors don't want to see me again for twelve months. I telephoned my wife and this is the second call I have made since I heard the good news. Thanks for the prayers, Andy,' he concluded.

Yet another phone call had left me with absolutely nothing to say. For the next five or ten minutes or so my firm received no value at all for the salary they were paying me as I sat dead still. But then on the credit side, my directors had an experienced executive back on the job much sooner than anyone anticipated.

Months later a travelling inspector of our organisation on a routine visit informed me that Paddy, our mutual colleague, had some weeks previously described to him our prayer session in hospital on that Friday night. Paddy told our inspector that at the

moment we put our hands together in prayer, he was conscious
of being surrounded by a warm glow and immediately knew he
was healed. Further, he stated, that he was not surprised when
all his tests proved negative on the following Monday – but the
doctors were.*

Interestingly enough, this warm glow described by my colleague
and of which I was totally unaware was to crop up again, shortly.

AN ELECTRIC FIRE OR. . ?

One Friday morning in my office I received an unusual telephone
call. It was from a lady who announced her name and stated she
was ringing from Naas. She had heard that a man named Andy
O'Neill prayed with sick people and wondered was she speaking
to the right person. I asked how she became aware of such knowledge and she replied that a friend of hers, who attended our prayer
meeting infrequently, told her so. The caller then outlined her
problem. Her sister Jane, sadly a terminal cancer victim on a visit
from London and who was flying out of Dublin Airport at 8 am
on the following Saturday morning would dearly love to meet me
for healing prayers. Jane realised that this could well be her last
visit to her family in Ireland. She said that the prognosis was that
her sister had only a matter of weeks to live. I explained that my
wife and I had a dinner date with friends that night and with Naas
being some thirty miles from Dublin, her proposition did not seem
feasible. Being a working chap I could not leave my office on that
very busy day so I said the only possibility was for herself and
her sister to drive from their home to meet me in Dublin, should
they so desire, and to make matters easy for them I suggested that
they might call to my office at 5 pm where we could have some
ten or fifteen minutes together before the arrival of the office
cleaners. I concluded that if such arrangements were unsuitable
or inconvenient for them, then that would have to be the end of
the matter. Much to my surprise, my caller agreed to the suggestion and having received directions as to the location of my office,
confirmed that her sister and herself would call to me as arranged.

As my office staff were leaving my two visitors arrived, both
looking very unsure and hesitant. Surely they found themselves

* This occurred in 1979. At the time of writing, 1984, Paddy is a very busy,
progressive executive.

in a most unusual position – arriving at an insurance office for prayers! Just to be where they were must have taken quite a bit of courage. I welcomed them, ushered both ladies into my office and arranged three chairs. The lady who was ill sat in the centre while her sister and I sat on either side of her. I told them briefly how I came to this healing business and some of the happenings which had occurred. Then I held out my hands and invited them to place their hands on mine. They did so and we praised the Lord together for the healing of Jane, read a few verses from Scripture from the Letter of St James and finished by reciting the Lord's prayer, Hail Mary and *Gloria*.

The session lasted about ten or fifteen minutes and ended with the arrival of the office cleaners. The sick lady appeared to be radiant with hope and confidence after the prayers and she said, 'I never felt so well for a long time and I now believe that this will not be my last visit to Ireland to see my family.' She then went on to tell us that during the prayers she had her eyes closed to assist her concentration but affirmed that a few moments after the prayers began, she was conscious of being surrounded by a warm glow. When I suggested that it must have been caused by the electric fire, she replied that it was not that sort of warmth! Apparently for her it was very real. Her face was aglow and her sister, looking at her, seemed to be astonished. I escorted these two very surprised ladies to their car and went home.

Some time later the lady from Naas rang and informed me that on arrival in London, Jane reported to her doctor and informed him that she felt very well. After tests and examination, the doctor informed his patient that apparently her condition had stabilised, all deterioration having ceased. Having no explanation to offer, her doctor laughingly suggested that her native air must have cured her!

It interested me to reflect on the warm glow which was experienced by the sick lady while we prayed in my office, this phenomenon having manifested itself a second time. But once again I was completely unaware of it, as was the sick lady's sister.*

* This incident happened in 1979. Jane attends her doctor in London every six months. He informed her, early in 1984, that many patients who had consulted him since her initial visit, had long since gone to the Lord. Jane, who plans to visit her sister in Naas for a holiday has asked her to arrange a celebratory lunch and to invite me to be their guest.

4

On the Job Training

Looking back on the period of my life which I have described so far, it is now easy for me to appreciate that the happenings which I had witnessed were random affairs. I was active in and dealing with situations in a haphazard manner. If these happenings were healings and if I had entered or stumbled into the Healing Ministry, well in business management terminology I could be classified as totally unskilled and lacking in elementary training in the theory and practice of Christian healing. For all I knew at that stage the term Healing Ministry could well have been pie-in-the-sky charismatic renewal exaggeration. But unknowingly I was heading for what is known in Management Institute jargon as 'On the Job Training' (Practical Section). The theory was to come much later. From a business management point of view, everything seemed to be happening in reverse order.

My first on the job training session began with the illness of a very good friend, Dick. He suffered a coronary and was hospitalised in an Intensive Care Unit. I had visited him once and now it had occurred to me to offer him this laying on of hands healing. I decided to extend to him the full treatment – the laying on of hands, the reading of Scripture, praying in tongues and the recitation of the Lord's prayer. I felt that now that I was seeing total strangers being healed by this (for me) new method, why not let my friends have the benefit of it?

So I planned my first visit to Dick and presented myself at the Intensive Care Unit reception area, some fifteen minutes before visiting hour. Being an insurance man I was confident I could talk my way in and once inside I would have a quarter of an hour by myself with him. Then undisturbed we could go through the whole healing routine as I understood it. So having bounced into the hospital with my Scripture under my arm, there I was, seeking permission to visit my friend. However there was some delay before he could be located and waiting for the nurse to return, I anxiously eyed my watch. Valuable time was being eaten into my planned precious fifteen minute period. Eventually a nurse returned and informed me that my friend had been discharged from the Intensive Care Unit to another section of the hospital! By the time I discovered Dick, his bed was surrounded by his family, friends and well wishers and the 'crack' was overpowering. My enthusiasm for healing him began to diminish and it finally evaporated. When I waved goodbye to him I doubt if he even saw me do so and I wandered disconsolately out into the hospital corridor.

Walking alone down that corridor, I endeavoured to establish the cause of my failure. Having neither tradition of, or training in, the Healing Ministry I realised that I had no guide lines. All I could do was try to apply my business management training know-how to the position. So I felt that as a raw newcomer to this healing craft, it could be expected that I would make elementary mistakes as I had no back up of skilled experienced tutors or mentors. Worse still, there was nobody with whom I could confer. However I knew that in my own business I had developed the ability to read the game as they say. I always knew what was going on in my firm and in the insurance industry generally and more importantly, I knew why. Therefore my business anticipatory sense was well known and respected by my colleagues and was possibly a self-preservation instinct too. That same know-how came to my rescue on the long walk down the hospital corridor. It dawned on me that I was rushing my fences and that the prudent thing to do now was to slow down the whole operation. Should I accept that I was in the healing ministry, then it was logical to assume that I was not using my own power. This being so, it automatically followed that the timing of any healing could never be anticipated by me. I had in fact stumbled across one of the basic principles of Christian healing – the timing of the healing must always be the Lord's. Applying this principle to the visit to Dick, my error became immediately apparent. I had decided to heal Dick. I had planned when and where the healing would take place. I had taken both control and responsibility for the whole affair. And nothing happened. I didn't even get started! Summing up then, in retrospect, it appeared to me as plain as daylight that it was my availability which was needed in the healing ministry,

not my ability. Without knowing it I was heading for freedom
and relaxation in the healing craft. Should I accept this newly
discovered principle then all responsibility would be removed
from me and with it would go any pressure to produce results.
My growing up, my unconscious quest for some sort of order and
maturity in the healing ministry, had begun. But two further
training sessions were to follow in the weeks and months ahead.

On the Monday evening following my visit to Dick I headed
unwittingly into the second session of on the job training in the
healing ministry. As I entered St Vincent's Hospital for my normal
Society of St Vincent de Paul work I decided to adopt a low
profile towards healing following my decision to slow things down.
My positive thinking strictly confined me to limit my action to
two areas: (1) to be among the sick, and (2) to be available.

And I left it so. I visited two patients and had relaxed chats
with each of them of approximately five minutes duration,
listening to their health worries and wishing them well. Leaving
them I entered another ward and was immediately greeted by two
ladies who were visitors. The three of us met regularly at the
Tuesday night prayer meeting. One of the ladies, Betty, said, 'Oh
praise the Lord, Andy, we knew you visit this hospital on Monday
nights and we were hoping that we would meet you. But with four
or five hundred patients here, we didn't think we had much chance
– but here you are!'

Resisting the temptation to remind them that they could have
simplified the matter by telephoning me I responded to their
greeting and warily enquired why they wished to see me. Betty,
introducing the patient said, 'Please Andy, lay your hands on Mary
for healing.'

I immediately shied away from the bed and replied, 'Let the
two of you lay your hands on her while I search for a patient who
has no visitor.'

But both my friends pleaded, 'Oh, please do, Andy.'

'I have no special hot line to the Holy Spirit. Go ahead
yourselves. We are all in this healing business together,' I said.

Then the patient spoke, simply saying, 'Please sir, lay your
hands on me and pray with me.'

I looked at her, being too busy with her two visitors to have
taken much notice of her previously and I saw a lovely old lady,
in her seventies I presumed. She was looking at me so hopefully

that I felt totally inadequate. Again she pleaded, holding out her hands, 'Please do sir.' The word 'sir' bowled me over, so I sat down at the side of her bed and told her that my name was Andy. But I thought here I was being drawn into the healing business again despite my week-old decision to cool things. But I compromised by agreeing to become involved provided all of us held hands and prayed together. Betty, her co-visitor Joan and the patient Mary joyfully agreed but I continued to play things in a very low key remembering my visit to Dick on the previous Monday night. Then Betty said, 'Andy, let me put you in the picture concerning Mary,' and she outlined the sick lady's story.

Mary, who was a widow, wished to travel to Australia, where her only child had recently emigrated with her husband and four children. She had sold her home in Dublin and wished to spend the rest of her life with her family in Australia. Mary had made three attempts to travel but on the eve of each departure date she invariably suffered a coronary and found herself in a coronary care unit instead of in Dublin Airport. Her doctors gave her very little hope of ever being strong enough to make the journey. There she was with all the necessary documentation passport, visa, resident permit, air ticket, accommodation guaranteed and adequate financial security – everything except the health and strength to get up and go.

Then the old lady spoke again, saying, 'I don't care how long I have to live, be it a few years, a few months or a few weeks – whatever time the Lord leaves me, I want to spend it with my grandchildren.'

Having listened to these words I was hooked and my prudence and the whole critical apparatus faded away. There at the bedside the four of us holdings hands, prayed together, asking the Holy Spirit to come into that situation with His healing power. When the prayers ended, we released our hands, all eight of them and the lovely dear old lady put her arms around me and kissed me. As I made my farewell these three ladies shared tears galore.

One week later, Betty, one of Mary's visitors, while attending the Tuesday night prayer meeting, described our encounter with the patient in St Vincent's Hospital. She said that after our visit Mary had an undisturbed night's sleep and woke the following morning feeling very well indeed. The doctors examined her, did some tests and decided to discharge her from the hospital on the following day. Mary had returned to her flat in Dublin and was doing fine, health-wise.

At the next Tuesday night prayer meeting Betty arrived with a cablegram. It was from our former patient Mary and was sent from Australia. It read 'Very enjoyable flight – stop – my grandchildren welcomed me at the aiport – stop – thanks for the prayers – stop – love to all – stop – Mary.'

I had learned in this on the job training session that to those engaged in the healing ministry, the power of the Holy Spirit may be seen to work, at times, in an unpredictable manner. This basic principle can be confirmed by reading the Scripture story of the Lord raising from the dead the only son of a widowed mother. Leaving Capernaum, the Lord was about to enter a town called Naim, when near the town gate he met a funeral. The only son of a widowed mother was dead. The stricken mother was following the funeral. There is no scriptural evidence that the mother ever pleaded with the Lord. Rather it would appear likely that she never even heard of him. The widow's son couldn't have asked the Lord for anything – he was dead. But the Lord stopped the funeral, raised the dead man to life and restored him to his mother in the twinkling of an eye – the unpredictable power of the Spirit of God.

So my get-up-and-go action in the healing ministry was now being supported with some little knowledge of the healing craft. But my on the job training programme was to continue when my coming into contact with another lady vividly demonstrated to me a further fundamental principle of Christian healing and left me with a memory which I will forever humbly cherish.

THE FINAL SOLUTION

On a warm summer's afternoon one of the most dramatic events of my life was about to begin, just as my day's work in the office was drawing to a close. It all began with a simple telephone call from a nun, a sister in a nursing order. She announced her name, Sister Mary, and said she understood that I prayed with the sick for healing adding that we met once casually. But I could not place her. The sister asked me would I be so kind as to visit and pray with a life long friend of hers who was seriously ill. The patient was in one of the Nursing Homes of the religious order to which the nun belonged. Once again I endeavoured to back off and suggested to the sister that she should do the praying herself. But the sister would have none of it and gently insisted that I should come and do the job. Playing for time I tried to outline to the good sister that after a life time of service to the Lord, surely her prayers would be much more efficacious than mine, a Johnny-come-lately to the healing business. But she would not entertain any of my suggestions and stuck to her guns continuing to ask me to come. With her background I knew she had no experience of the techniques of telephone selling but she made a sale with me, her quiet insistance eventually winning the day. Finally I acquiesced and then asked the sister when did she wish me to see the patient. The reply came back, 'Please, Mr O'Neill, come now!'

I checked the time, it was 4.50 pm, so I said, 'I pass your nursing home on my way home. I should be with you in about fifteen minutes.' The sister thanked me and said she already knew where I lived and this knowledge assisted her in deciding the best time to contact me! We put down the telephones and I realised that I had just spoken to a very intelligent woman.

I had arranged to meet the sister at the reception desk of the Nursing Home and there I was greeted by a middle-aged nun whom I recognised. We had spoken to each other some days previously while waiting to enter a lift. The nun informed me that the sick lady and herself were life long friends but while Sister Mary adhered to the principle of medical confidentiality, I gathered that the patient's complaint was very, very serious indeed. But prognosis or diagnosis was not my field. I was simply in the healing ministry. When Sister Mary asked how I was going to approach the patient I only then realised that the nun had acted on her own in contacting me, the patient having no prior knowledge of my impending visit.

So with all the brash confidence of an insurance man and some little hope in the Lord's power, I replied that I didn't know what I was going to do or say, adding that I was on the Lord's work and would turn the whole visit over to Him. But what I didn't know was that the patient knew exactly what she was going to do and say!

Sister Mary ushered me into a ward and introduced me to her friend. The atmosphere was quite stiff and formal as the patient was obviously sizing me up and wondering why a complete stranger was visiting her. Deciding that there was no point in beating about the bush, I made my submission without further ado. I simply said, 'Hilda, I praise the Lord with a charismatic renewal prayer group and I find myself in what is termed the healing ministry.'

That was as far as I got. Hilda raised herself up in the bed and said, 'Straight away let me tell you I want no contact whatsoever with anyone in this Charismatic Renewal affair. I don't want people turning my notions and ideas of God upside down. And that's final.' I stood up immediately and said I totally understood her position, thanked her for receiving me, wished her well and withdrew from the ward followed by the nun. Poor Sister Mary was visibly embarrassed and apologised profusely as we made for the lift.

But being an insurance man of many years standing I don't bruise easily. Anyhow I had long since accepted that the wishes and welfare of a patient must always be of primary and paramount importance and in no way should anybody in the healing ministry ever disturb a patient. So I reassured the sister that there was no harm done but seeing that I was in the Nursing Home I asked would she be interested in adjourning to the oratory with me to pray for the healing of Hilda. There we held hands and interceded with the Lord to heal Hilda. Not having the gift of bi-location, we asked the Lord to accept our hands on each other as our hands on Hilda, and to lay His merciful healing hands on her. We spent fifteen minutes in prayer and finished by reading a few verses of Scripture. This was about the length of time I was prepared to spend with Hilda should she have accepted my visit. At the end of our session Sister Mary remarked how she wished her community could pray as freely and in such an uninhibited manner. Jokingly I reminded her that I would not become involved in radically altering the prayer style of her Order. The complications of the healing ministry was quite enough, as I had just experienced. So I made my farewell and went home.

At precisely 4.50 pm the next day, while at my desk at work, Sister Mary telephoned me again. She said, 'Please, Andy, come and visit Hilda. Everything is all right now.'

'You must be joking, Sister. Why, I was thrown out yesterday and once bitten twice shy.'

But the nun insisted, 'Please, Andy, do come.'

'No way, Sister. Healing in the name of the Lord can't be forced or sold. In my view, it doesn't work that way,' I countered. But she continued to plead with me. Again I declined, saying, 'I tried in my own way to talk to that lady yesterday but she would have none of it and told me so quite plainly, as you heard yourself. And the best of luck to her. It is her life and she has a right to decide who should visit her and who shouldn't – and I'm in the latter category.' But the nun persisted saying, 'Hilda just did not understand what your mission was all about and would simply love to see you. Please come, Andy,' she pleaded, 'otherwise she will be very upset. She is asking me all day to contact you and believe me, it has taken no little courage for me to telephone you again.'

God forgive me, I felt myself weakening and said, 'All right then, I'll come,' adding, 'when would you say I should call?' And back came the answer, 'Please come now, Andy. I will be waiting for you and will bring you to her.' Suddenly the conversation was over and I remember saying to myself that I must be out of my mind to accept that invitation again.

However I drove to the Nursing Home, was met by Sister Mary and we entered Hilda's ward together. Her whole face lit up when she saw us and began, 'Please forgive me for yesterday. I just didn't understand.' So straight away the good nun, the patient and I held hands as I endeavoured to explain in a few words the central idea of the healing mission. My goodness, it was like pushing an open door. There was no resistance from Hilda who was now totally receptive to the message of the Lord, even allowing for the Word being sent forth so inadequately and inexpertly by me. But it was a lovely session of prayer lasting some ten minutes. When the praise and prayer ended, Hilda seemed somehow consoled and Sister Mary's face exuded joy. Promising to keep in touch, I then left and was home in good time for the family evening meal.

Over a period of some months I kept in constant touch with Hilda, calling once and sometimes twice a week. One day I even called on my way home from the harmless tennis I play, clad in a red track suit and tennis shoes. I bounced into the ward saying, 'Anyone for tennis?' in an effort to lift her spirits and bring a touch of the outside world to her bedside. Hilda always seemed so glad to see me and loved the prayers for her recovery. During one of

my visits I met her husband, Jack, who received me and the idea
of the healing ministry very kindly and I also met several members
of her family from time to time. So quite a large family circle
heard of the aims and objects of the healing ministry of the
Charismatic Renewal Movement. But Hilda's health continued to
deteriorate. Then one evening as I was about to enter the ward a
nurse called me and suggested that I limit my visit to two minutes.
Hilda's life was drawing to a close. I visited her and a flicker of
recognition appeared in her eyes for a moment, with a trace of a
smile. I prayed silently and then in deference to the medical
instructions, left quickly.

The following morning before leaving for work I telephoned
the Nursing Home to be informed that Hilda went home to the
Lord during the night. She was dead and I was shattered. It was
the first time I had met death while active in the healing mission.
Driving to the office that morning I reviewed the whole situation
from the day I was first invited to visit her to the day of her death.
And I couldn't understand the reason why the Lord had allowed
me to be brought into it. There I was, I mused, sitting at my desk
minding my own business when the telephone rang, not once but
twice, to bring me to Hilda. Surely the Lord knew that Hilda was
not to be healed. He knew that her sickness was to end in death.
I didn't. What kind of Christian witness did I show to her husband
and members of her family, I wondered, now that she was dead?
What did they think of the man and what he represented, who
was so constantly at her bedside saying, 'Jesus Christ heals' and
Jesus Christ said, 'Heal the sick'? Suddenly I became unsure of
the whole healing ministry and my approach to and understanding
of it. So at Mass on the morning of Hilda's death I had a head-to-
head confrontation with the Lord. 'Lord,' I said, 'I must have the
healing ministry all wrong. I'm sure I have the wrong end of the
stick. Here I was led into a situation to pray for the recovery of
Hilda and now she is dead.' So there and then I made a very firm,
no nonsense, offer to the Lord. I told him that in no way could I
understand the position and if I was to continue in the healing
ministry then this whole mystery of Hilda's death needed to be
cleared up, spelled out and explained to me, otherwise my days
in the healing ministry were at an end. I wanted a direct word
from the Lord. I had accepted that whenever we prayed with a
sick person for healing, then a healing of some sort or other took

place. I had to accept this fact because I had read in His living word that we always receive when we ask. Where was the healing in Hilda's death? I couldn't see it or explain it so I concluded that in the absence of a direct word or explanation from the Lord, then Andy O'Neill was from that day forth finished in the healing ministry. Mass ended and I went to work.

But the day passed with no word from the Lord or anyone else. I hadn't a clue as to how it would come but I was determined that should I not receive it then I would take it that such absence would indicate that I was no longer needed in the healing ministry. The day after Hilda's death came and still no word. So walking to lunch to a nearby hotel I mused that this day might well see the end of my involvement in the healing ministry and possibly in the whole Charismatic Renewal Movement as well. I entered the restaurant of the hotel and had lunch, all alone. I finished my meal, paid the bill and was walking towards the exit when I heard a man's voice call, 'Andy.' I turned and there coming to meet me was Hilda's husband Jack! He was also in the restaurant with his family but I did not see him while I was there. Before I had time to say a word he said, 'I am so delighted to see you, Andy.'

'Hilda is dead, Jack,' I replied.

'She is, Andy, and I have just come from her burial,' he said sadly.

'But I prayed so often for Hilda's recovery and now she is dead,' I said.

'Andy,' he simply said, 'you came into Hilda's life for the last few months of her stay on earth. You will never appreciate the consolation and joy your visits brought to her. You never knew how much she looked forward to your coming and the peace and tranquillity she experienced when you left.' Then he concluded, 'Andy, myself and my whole family will never be able to repay you for all you did for Hilda.' With that he put his arms around me, there in the middle of the hotel lobby and said just two words 'Thanks Andy.' He turned and went back to his family leaving me flat footed and motionless.

Hilda's husband never knew where I lived or worked nor did I know where he lived or worked. But walking back to the office that day I thought of all the endless permutations which one could number concerning the chances of both of us meeting. There were for instance so many other restaurants and hotels to which he could have gone on that day. There were even four separate departments where meals were served in the hotel where we met, and in all my years of patronage of that hotel I had never seen Hilda's husband in any of them. I also realised that on that memorable day for me, my business duties could have taken me far away from that hotel. But then one could go on and on. Anyway, for my money, I was sure that a word had come directly from the Lord to me as I asked. I couldn't have come closer than contacting Hilda's husband on the very day of her burial.

Surely in this whole experience I had again stumbled across a further basic principle of Christian healing. I had been taught that in the healing ministry one is always faced with the prospect of the death of the patient. But it had now been confirmed to me that the healing power of the Lord is made manifest in mysterious ways even when death comes. On that sad but never to be forgotten day for me I knew I was locked into the healing ministry and committed permanently to the Charismatic Renewal Movement because of the death of a lovely person. I gratefully and humbly thanked the Lord for bringing me to Hilda's bedside during the last few months of her life. I asked the Lord to bless and console her husband and family and take them safely through their sad days. I was sure that Hilda was with the Lord – there was no place else for her to go. The memory of a lovely woman, whose surname I never knew, I will treasure, gratefully, always.

5

Out and About

The Tuesday night prayer meetings continued to be a great escape from the pressures of life for me. Every Tuesday I looked forward so much to this gathering of friends and invariably returned home from it refreshed in mind and physically relaxed. But quite suddenly it all ended. The core group (or committee) of the prayer meeting, in their wisdom, decided that it was time to move on from the public meeting concept and began to form small communities of people who would meet weekly for prayer in their own homes on a rotational basis. These communities consisted of from six to eight people in each unit, all of whom were withdrawn from the public Tuesday night prayer meeting. The attendance at the prayer meeting declined accordingly.

However, I was not drawn to this new idea of becoming part of one of these small communities and, furthermore, some members of the core group considered that I had an inordinate concentration on the healing ministry. Inevitably there was a confrontation and I found myself dramatically and suddenly with no place to go, Charismatic Renewal-wise, on a Tuesday night. I will forever remember the first Tuesday night, when instead of gathering my Scripture and driving joyfully with great expectations to the prayer meeting venue, I found myself in the garden, cutting grass. The sense of loss was so real that it was difficult for me to get through that Tuesday night without it. But I continued to mow the grass and praise the Lord and accepted that Tuesday nights would never be quite the same again. But to survive in life, one must be constantly prepared to pick oneself up off the floor and begin again. So rather then moping over days which were gone, I began straight away to review my new position and to apply the positive thinking attitude developed in my business management training to the void left in my life by the loss of the weekly prayer meeting.

Naturally enough, I discussed the whole position with friends
of mine who were in the Renewal and who attended prayer meetings in other parts of Dublin. I knew I needed to attach myself
to another prayer meeting but the trick was to find one in a convenient venue. Joe FitzPatrick, that very good friend of mine,
suggested that I should take a look at one which was held every
Wednesday evening in 'Avila', the Carmelite Monastery in
Morehampton Road. The venue was most attractive to me as it
was a very short distance from my new office in Dartmouth Square
on the Grand Canal and close to the Burlington Hotel. I reckoned
I could have an evening meal in that hotel on a Wednesday, proceed
to the Carmelite Monastery nearby and, after the prayer meeting,
return home conveniently on through Donnybrook to my home
in Blackrock.

So some weeks after my withdrawl from the Tuesday night
prayer meeting, I decided to push my luck and go in search of
'Avila'. Having finished work I enjoyed an evening meal in the
Burlington Hotel and with all the confidence of an insurance salesman found myself in the grounds of 'Avila' walking through the
beautiful grounds there. I was amazed at the peace and the silence
of the scene, just a stone's throw away from the non-stop noise of
one of the country's busiest roads. The only thing moving in this
place was a man jogging. I called him and enquired as to the
whereabouts of a prayer meeting. He pointed to a small door in
the great building and said, 'There you go,' and continued his
jogging. I followed instructions and went through the door and
found a beautifully furnished hall where people were gathering.
Some were arranging chairs in a circular fashion in the
manner of Charismatic Renewal prayer meetings, when a man
recognising I was a stranger came to me and said, 'You are very
welcome to our prayer meeting.' I had an extraordinary feeling
that I had come home.

The hall quickly filled with people, the prayer meeting began,
and I just sat there gratefully. I was in, accepted without question
and none of the good people there asked who I was or where I
came from. I just couldn't believe my luck. The prayer meeting
ended and I fled to my car, fearful that the whole experience was
a dream. But I remember singing joyfully in tongues as I drove
all the way along the Stillorgan Road that night. When I arrived
home, my wife Delia said, 'Well Andy, you must have had a good

day at the office.' Certainly I had had a good day – a very, very good day. My astonishing confrontation with the Charismatic Renewal movement which began on a Tuesday night had now moved to Wednesday nights but the action which up to now had been confined to Dublin, was about to spread further afield to far away places with strange sounding names.

RING A RING A ROSEY

It was holiday time again and on a Saturday morning in September my wife and I boarded an Aer Lingus jet at Dublin Airport bound for our island in the sun. Rhodes was our destination. It was an interesting but tiring daylight flight. After touchdown we were thankful that the bus journey to our hotel was a short one. We settled quickly into our rooms, had dinner and retired early, looking forward to the two weeks precious break.

After breakfast on the following Sunday morning our party assembled in the hotel lobby awaiting transport to Mass. After a delay of some ten or fifteen minutes it became apparent that it was difficult to find a courier and also the exact location of a Catholic Church and the times of Mass were not readily forthcoming. A Catholic priest had travelled with the party but the word was that he had no intention of acting as chaplain to the group so would not entertain the idea of celebrating Mass in the hotel that morning, which would have solved our problem on the spot. The priest considered that being on holiday in a private capacity, he had no commitment Mass-wise to anybody, which was fair enough. Members of our party, were scattered around the lobby chatting together, seeking information. I was prowling around like a caged lion, as the time dragged on, restlessly seeking news at the reception desk or from the various groups of fellow travellers. I simply wanted transport to the church to get Mass over and done with as quickly as possible. With all due respect to the Lord, I had come to Rhodes for sand, sun and sea and just fifty yards from our hotel there in full view was the beach with its golden sun drenched sand, edged with inviting endless waves of surf. I was reminded of my childhood days when I sometimes stood gazing into a sweet shop window with no money in my pocket.

Suddenly I found myself chatting to a man and his wife, who like myself had no idea as to how our Mass problem was to be solved. We introduced ourselves and discovered that although we only lived about a mile apart in Dublin, we had never met previously. Upsets and difficulties are not uncommon on the package deal holiday scene, and there we were, seemingly stuck with this problem. So without more ado, I informed my two friends that to solve the whole mess, I was, there and then, going to bring the power of the praising of God into this confused situation. Both of them showed immediate interest and no little surprise at this approach so I informed them of my involvement in the Charismatic Renewal Movement and of our constant use of expectant faith in every situation. The solution to our problem seemed simple to me. Without the services of a courier or transport and still with no knowledge of the location of a Catholic church or Mass times, the obvious way out of the difficulty seemed that a second approach should be made to the priest who was on the hotel premises and once again request him to oblige us. So a deputation was selected to contact him and hearing of it, I told my two friends that I was now praising God that the priest would consent. Still transportless and courierless, we awaited the result of the deputation, as I continued silently to praise the Lord. At last our deputation returned and requested our party to immediately assemble in the hotel ballroom. Our priest had changed his mind and had now agreed to celebrate Mass. By lift and stairway we headed for the ballroom with my two friends slightly shocked at the way the position had been turned around after hours of indecision and confusion. I offered to read the lesson at Mass for the priest. He consented and at the conclusion of Mass I led a round of applause for his kindness to us. Insurance salesmen do not miss many tricks! The priest responded in some style, by inviting us all to join with him in the Breaking of Bread every morning for the next two weeks at 10 am in the hotel ballroom. Not alone had we got our Sunday Mass but in effect we had suddenly been given the gift of a personal chaplain for every day of the holiday.

Within fifteen minutes of the ending of that Sunday Mass, I was in the sea under cloudless skies, celebrating life and praising God with every swimming stroke.

That evening, Delia and I, with two friends of many years standing, Mary and Tony, together with the couple we had met for the first time that morning, Denis and Eileen, all sat down to dinner. Discussing the manner in which our Mass problem had been solved, my observation that the praising of God had released some power into the situation and possibly resulted in the priest changing his mind, caused some friendly leg pulling and merriment. But unknown to us a scene was about to be set, where all six of us assembled at that dinner table were to be concerned in, and witness to, a simply extraordinary happening.

We were enjoying a wonderful holiday in Rhodes. Our hotel was spacious, well furnished and immaculately clean. The food, from a European point of view, was first class and the swimming pool and gardens were most attractive, and the views from the hotel were awe-inspiring. With good company and wonderful weather, what more could we ask? So on the first Monday morning of our holiday the six of us who had dined sumptuously the previous evening were on the beach on loungers and under sun umbrellas. We changed into swimming togs and headed into the beautiful sea. It was a magnificent swim with the blue water as clear as glass. We returned to our beach loungers and towelling ourselves on the hot sand in brilliant sunshine – life seemed just perfect. At that moment I was sure that none of us would have changed the scene for any place on earth. Then I noticed Eileen and Denis whispering together in a very agitated manner. After a few minutes, Denis sat down disconsolately while Eileen came to us with the sad news. Seemingly, Denis, on coming out of the sea, stumbled and put down his hands into the sea and sand to save himself from falling. He continued up the beach but while towelling himself suddenly noticed that his wedding ring had disappeared from his left hand. The ring which his wife Eileen had so lovingly slipped on his finger on their wedding day had been lost in the sea. In Eileen's own words, the incident was enough to ruin their holiday. I immediately offered to go to the spot where Denis had stumbled to look for the ring but Eileen declined my offer saying that Denis was so upset that any commotion would only exacerbate the situation. My offer to search was an automatic reaction and was more hopeful than realistic. Now the one small drawback on the beach was that on entering the water one had to walk over small sharp stones which stretched outwards for some six to eight yards. But once outside that zone one trod on firm stoneless sand. But walking on those stones while getting in to swim and coming out was a painful experience for the few seconds involved.

We surveyed the scene with the waves surging and churning countless thousands of small stones, sand and seaweed onto the beach in a never ending crescendo of sound. Some twelve miles away as one looked out to sea was the coastline of Turkey, plainly visible. Somewhere in there was Denis' wedding ring. Eileen and I just stood there in silence and sadness as I pondered how amazingly quickly any worldly scene can change. Then Eileen turned to me and said something which quite shocked me, 'Andy, isn't it in situations like this that you Charismatic Renewal people praise the Lord?'

'Yes, Eileen, we can bring the power of the praising of God into any situation,' I replied, hesitantly, realising the magnitude of the problem – a ring lost in the sea. 'Will you praise the Lord for this one?' she asked.

'Certainly,' I said, and we did so on the beach there and then. But for me that was the end of the matter.

We idled away that lazy summer's day on the beach, had a light snack at lunch time in a nearby cafe, returned to our hotel in the late afternoon and changed for dinner, after which we went our separate ways.

On Tuesday morning as usual Delia and I went down to breakfast in the very spacious hotel restaurant. It was very early and we were almost alone there when suddenly we saw Eileen enter and approach us. Her face bore the look of total astonishment and bewilderment, so much so that I never will forget it. She sat down at our table and told us her story. That morning she rose even earlier than Delia and I and went by herself to the beach which was entirely deserted. She took off her shoes and entered the sea at the place where she thought her husband had stumbled the previous morning when he had lost his ring. She praised the Lord and put her left hand into the sea, sand and stones until her wrist was covered. She then closed the fingers of her hand and drew it up. She opened it and there in the middle of the sand, stones and dripping sea water, in her hand, shone her husband's wedding ring! Thereupon Eileen, at our breakfast table opened her hand and in it we saw Denis' wedding band. Delia and I were speechless. For me that was the end of my breakfast as Eileen departed.

That evening all six of us, who had witnessed the loss of the ring on the previous Monday morning and who had shared the sadness of it, sat down to a celebration dinner. Later that night

while my wife Delia was playing Bridge, I read a chapter of the
Acts of the Apostles and after the finding of Denis' ring I could
identify more than ever before with the signs and wonders which
followed St Paul on his travels. There is abundant scriptural and
historical evidence of Paul's journeys to Rhodes and maybe I
thought, while here on holiday, we are even walking the very
ground he trod on. Then I recalled the words of some of my
friends in the Renewal at home in Dublin, who insisted that we
should constantly expect signs and wonders when we praise the
Lord. They maintained that we, in this age, are experiencing the
second pentecost. It is said that nobody would have recognised
the first Pentecost but for its signs and wonders.

But the finding of the ring had an astonishing affect on our
whole party. Almost every one of its one hundred and twenty
members came to me during the holiday at some time or another
and spoke to me of the Lord, on the beach, in the hotel, in discos,
in bars and on tours. Most were perplexed and I remembered a
teaching given at a prayer meeting where it was outlined that signs
and wonders are an embarrassment to Christians who hold that
the age of miracles is past. Some of the party even asked me was
the whole thing a put up job or a practical joke. I responded by
pointing out that one would hardly be into the practical joke scene
with two people within a few minutes of meeting them for the
first time.

Seeing is believing, as they say, and Denis wore his wedding
ring more proudly then ever before during the remainder of the
holiday. But every other time he went swimming he left his ring
safely in his hold-all on the beach.

All good things come to an end and after two weeks on our
island in the sun our holiday party assembled in the airport at
Rhodes, awaiting the arrival of an Aer Lingus jet. The joy of
anticipation, which was so evident at Dublin airport on our holiday
eve, was now replaced by a sense of satisfaction that we were going
home, so much so that when the shamrock bedecked jet landed,
a cheer went up from the Irish gathered in the airport viewing
lounge. Just then, a man, a member of our party came to me and
told me of his inordinate fear of flying. In his hand were two
tablets. He informed me that coming out his instructions were
to take one tablet an hour before departure and to swallow the
other immediately at take-off. And he did so. On the flight out

from Dublin he was served a meal and drink with the rest of the party. He disembarked at Rhodes, boarded a bus, and somewhere between Rhodes airport and the hotel he suddenly became aware of where he was. He was shocked to realise that he had no recollection of the flight. I assumed at first that he was having me on or maybe had a few drinks too many but he assured me that he was deadly serious as he looked with evident fright at the two pills in his hand. 'Andy', he continued, 'you praise the Lord in many situations – could you help me overcome this horrible fear of flying? I am terrified to take these tablets.' I told him that I was simply an insurance man with no knowledge of or skill in the use of tablets, pills or drugs, adding that in no way would I even comment on whether or not he should take his medicine. But I informed him that with his consent, I was prepared to lay my hands on him there and then in the airport lounge, to seek for him total freedom from the fear of flying by bringing the power of the praising of God into the situation. He consented, so we put our hands on each other's shoulders and praised the Lord for some ten seconds or so. He thanked me and we parted. An hour or so later, our party was summoned to a numbered exit gate, the message booming out over the public address system. This announcement was greeted with a cheer as the Irish rushed for that gate like rugby forwards charging for the line. There was no mistaking the fact that the Irish were going home!

I never saw that man afterwards, either on the plane or at Dublin airport on our return there. Some weeks later, however, I received a letter from him in which he told me that he had boarded the plane at Rhodes with the two tablets still in his hands. He kept them there for about half an hour after take off and then slowly put the two tablets, one by one, into the top pocket of his jacket.

He confirmed that he had enjoyed every moment of the flight but this time he remembered the meal and the drink served to him on the flight home and didn't need to be told of them by his travelling companion! He lives many miles from Dublin and concluded his letter by informing me that he had made contact with (as he put it) his local unit of the Charismatic Renewal Movement. On reading his letter I recalled the story of the bishop on his way to Vatican II, who on hearing the pilot's announcement that the aircraft was flying at 30,000 feet straightaway cancelled his order for a gin and tonic. Apparently he realised that he was too close to Head Office!

The thought of returning to the office on the Monday morning after a two week vacation and viewing the accumulated problems on one's desk is the stuff of which an insurance Area Manager's nightmare is made. But with the coming of the Praising of God into my life this terror was no more. So, in my office on the first Monday morning after my Rhodes holiday, with head down, working and praising the Lord, my desk was cleared at lunch time. Maybe, I reflected, as I leisurely strolled to the Burlington Hotel for lunch, I was getting a glimpse of that new life which my friends in the Renewal constantly claimed they enjoyed.

I now realised that the happenings which I had in the beginning, experienced exclusively in Dublin, had now spread to Rhodes. But the scene of a beautiful event was soon to be set in a place other than Dublin's fair city and occurred some weeks after my return from holiday.

SEEING IS BELIEVING

It all began in the Burlington Hotel one day at lunch with my friend Joe FitzPatrick when we were joined by a mutual friend, Dermot, who lives in the midlands. Being in the Renewal we were discussing the affairs of the three prayer meetings which we separately attended. Dermot informed us that he was a member of the core group of a newly-formed Charismatic Renewal prayer meeting in his home town and would welcome some support. He invited us to visit his prayer group, so having reviewed our engagements, we agreed on a date. Then on Monday afternoon, at the end of the day's work, Joe picked me up at my office and we headed by car to fulfil our promise. Once we cleared the city traffic and reached the Naas dual carriageway, we began singing the praises of the Lord. What a strange life I had been called to, I reflected – two grown men, driving along a road, praising God! I opened my scripture and read a passage or two aloud and the time went by so quickly that we hardly noticed the journey.

The venue of the prayer meeting was a private house, where a group of nuns had taken up residence. Each of the community was at work in the town, either teaching, home nursing or housekeeping for families in distress. As visitors we were entertained to an evening meal, following which a strange sight met our eyes.

All the furniture in the largish sitting room, with the exception of chairs and couches, was removed to the upper floor of the house by members of the community and friends who had just drifted in. It semed that a larger than usual crowd was expected. People began to arrive, were greeted, sat down and soon all the chairs in the house were brought to the sitting room to accommodate them. Eventually I found myself, like many others, sitting on the floor and when the meeting began, people were sitting in the hallway, on the stairs and on the landing. There was a full house for the Lord that night, I assure you and for some unknown reason an extraordinary sense of expectation and excitement prevailed.

The meeting progressed in the usual way and both Joe and I gave testimony to the happenings which we had witnessed in the Charismatic Renewal movement. At the conclusion of the meeting a group of us made ourselves available to anyone who wished to be prayed with, offering to lay our hands on them, should they so desire. Some people mentioned specific requests while others simply asked for prayers as they themselves silently communicated with the Lord. Needless to say, either approach was unquestionably acceptable to those of us in that small ministering group.

One lady came to be prayed with and asked for healing. She was on crutches, which she handed to friends while a few of us gathered around her. Jokingly I remarked that with the crush of people in the room, it would be impossible for her to fall now that she was crutchless. All I remember of that particular encounter was its joyfulness, the crippled lady smiling all the while as we praised God together. The prayers finished, she collected her crutches, thanked us and left with her friends. Shortly afterwards Joe and I said goodbye to our hosts and returned home.

The next day I was at lunch in the Burlington Hotel, when Dermot, who had set up the visit to his prayer group, joined me. He seemed extraordinarily elated and without more ado said that he had driven from Carlow especially to meet me – a journey of some fifty miles. 'Andy,' he said, 'I will tell you the story as it was told to me.' Dermot is a company representative and on that Tuesday morning he drove from his home to Carlow to make his usual calls. There he was contacted by telephone by one of the nuns in whose house we had met the previous night who informed him that the lady with the crutches, with whom we had prayed, called to the community house that morning, walking perfectly without crutches. It seemed that when the crippled lady left the prayer meeting, she walked with the aid of her crutches towards her home with her friends. However having walked some fifty yards or so she suddenly felt that she did not need the crutch in her right hand and handed it to one of her friends. Then having walked another few yards she decided she did not need the other crutch either and handed it to another friend and completed her journey home without any crutches. On entering her house she next discovered that the sight which she had lost in one eye had been restored. Naturally there was great rejoicing among her friends and neighbours. Her medical history was that some seven years previously she had suffered a stroke, losing the sight of one eye. Both legs were also affected so badly that she had to use a walking aid around the house and crutches whenever she left the house. So after the prayer meeting she had no further need of her crutches or her walking aid and could now see again out of both eyes.

When Joe and I prayed with her we had no knowledge of her medical condition or history. Actually we had not even seen her in the room until she arrived in front of us on crutches.

Dermot hearing that story by telephone in Carlow was so delighted that, rather than have his lunch there, he drove the fifty miles to Dublin to share the good news with me. I was astonished to hear the story but the look of shocked surprise was still on Dermot's face although he had heard the news some hours previously.

Twelve months later Joe and I again visited that prayer meeting in the midlands. The venue had moved now to a very spacious hall to accommodate the numbers attending. As we entered the hall a lady walked very smartly towards us from the other end of the hall. She welcomed us and said, 'Do you remember me?'

Neither of us could recall meeting her.

'The last time I met you both I was on crutches,' she explained. The three of us held hands and praised the Lord for his goodness. Certainly her joy was infectious.

Some time later I discussed this happening with Joe, remembering how we had set out to visit that prayer meeting where we met the crippled lady. Now she was crippled no more. Joe casually remarked, 'Isn't there something in Scripture where the Lord sent out seventy people, two by two and when they returned to him they said they had seen many signs and wonders? Andy, we will have to face the fact that this lady was healed in some way by the praising of God in that prayer meeting and by the laying on of hands in the name of Jesus Christ.' Dare we call it a healing, we wondered?

I had a lot yet to learn of the theory of Christian healing but I had seemingly entered a new phase. The healings or happenings were to continue in the future, but now they were about to happen when I was in the company of others – when we went out two by two, by invitation, to visit the sick in the name of the Lord.

THE DOCTORS' DILEMMA

Following the change of venue of my prayer meeting, I quickly established a new routine on Wednesdays. When the day's work ended, I would enjoy an evening meal at the Burlington Hotel, from where I would move on to the Carmelite foundation, 'Avila', and from there head home out on the Stillorgan Road at the end of the prayers. So that pattern of events cosily took care of Wednesday evenings.

One Wednesday, however, my routine changed with the arrival of my friend, Joe, at my office at the close of business. He asked me could I spare an hour or so and accompany him to a north city hospital to visit a student who was very ill. The sick boy's father, a business executive working in the city centre, had met Joe the previous day at a business lunch and told him of his son's illness. Apparently the illness began when the young man returned home from college, early one day, complaining of being unwell. He went to bed immediately but as his condition did not improve the family doctor was called in two days later. The doctor did not make much of the complaint and on hearing that the patient was suffering from mild pains in his legs, diagnosed a 'flu virus. He wrote a prescription and assured the patient that he should be up and about within three or four days. The doctor did not think that a second call would be necessary. Unfortunately the patient's condition worsened and the pains in his legs spread to his arms and became more pronounced and constant. Then on leaving his bed to walk to the bathroom the student collapsed and the doctor was called immediately. On seeing the boy's condition he rang a hospital and drove the patient to the casualty department where, after examination, he was admitted. During the next few days all the routine checks were carried out but the illness could not be diagnosed. The patient's condition continued to worsen and he eventually slipped into a coma. The family was shocked to see him in such a condition considering that a few weeks previously he had enjoyed good health. As he had spent a short holiday in the Middle East that summer, the full range of tropical disease tests were completed but were all negative. His condition baffled the doctors.

During a business lunch with the student's father, Joe introduced into the conversation the phenomenon of the Charismatic Renewal and its healing ministry to ascertain whether or not praying for healing would be acceptable to the family. Joe's offer to pray was accepted on the spot so Joe arranged an appointment to attend the hospital. His call to me was to invite me to accompany him on that Wednesday afternoon. So once again I found myself in Joe's car, driving across the city at peak traffic time, heading for a hospital. Unknown to me, this scene of two men in a car crossing Dublin city to visit the sick, while praising the Lord, was to repeat itself many times in the months ahead.

As we approached the hospital, cars were around us like flies around an open jar of jam in a garden. There wasn't a parking place in sight. We stopped the car and praised the Lord for somewhere to park when a man came up to us and said, 'Go forward a few yards, lads, I'm leaving and you can park here.' So we were parked and in the hospital within minutes. We met the student's father at the reception area, as arranged, Joe introduced him to me and all three of us went to the Intensive Care Unit. We arrived at the patient's side to find a doctor in attendance. The doctor just said two words, 'No change,' and left.

The sick boy was twenty years of age and was a fine, big, good-looking lad. But there he was unconscious. The three of us put our hands gently on him and praised the Lord. Joe read aloud, but quietly, a few verses of Scripture from the Letter of St James and also read the story from the Acts of the Apostles where Peter and John cured the crippled man, in the name of the Lord, outside the beautiful gate of the Temple. It was a quiet time in that Unit so we were undisturbed in prayer for about twenty minutes or so. When the prayers ended I recall saying to the patient's father, 'Well, that's it – that is as much as we can do,' or some similar remark, when suddenly the boy opened his eyes and began to talk.

His speech was incoherent, his father was startled but the young man had come out of the coma. The medical staff were called and Joe and I left the Unit. The father joined us within minutes, elated. He was oozing confidence as he proclaimed that he was satisfied that his son was now on the way to recovery for the first time since his illness began. He thanked us for coming, we parted and went our different ways as I made for the Burlington Hotel and my evening meal.

The following night Joe telephoned me at my home to say that the patient's family had contacted him with the news that their son was improving by the hour. Some days later the student was discharged with a clean bill of health but the nature of his illness has never been diagnosed.*

Shortly afterwards, over lunch, Joe and I were discussing the whole case. The fact was that we went out to visit a sick man, in the name of the Lord, with the sole intention of healing him and saw him, with our own eyes, come out of the coma after we had praised the Lord. But we knew just enough concerning divine healing, at this stage, to realise that a sick person may recover in four main ways:

(1) by the recuperative powers of mind and body;
(2) by medical and nursing skill;
(3) by the love of family and friends; and
(4) by the power of the Holy Spirit.

Viewed objectively then, we concluded that a sick person may get well by one or other of these four ways or even by a combination of some or all of them. Therefore, we accepted that even when we witness what appears to be an instant healing, in no way can we scientifically say that by the power of the Holy Spirit and by prayer alone has that healing taken place.

But who cares how a sick person recovers? However we agreed that when we minister to the sick and have the good fortune to see a healing whether it be instant or gradual, we would rejoice in the Lord, rather then spend time in teasing out the whys and the wherefores of the healing. After all, being a pair of working chaps, we had only very limited time to spend in the healing ministry. Mind you, we did acknowledge, though, that when all is said and done, to witness an instant healing when laying hands

* This event occurred in 1982. The young man has not had a moment's illness since.

on the sick in the name of the Lord is an astonishing experience. Strangly enough, for me these happenings were to continue, in the presence of other people, in situations organised by them.

WORLD CUP SOCCER

It was world cup time again and on a Wednesday afternoon in sunny Spain, England was due to play France. The match was to be shown live on television at 4.30 pm and as I hurried to the office on that morning, I promised myself to work as hard and as fast as possible, and be home in time to see the game. Spurred on by this aim, my work rate must have been very high indeed and my passion for soccer was so intense that I even cut out my usual coffee break.

Then at around eleven o'clock I received a telephone call. It was from John, a friend of mine. Both of us were in the Renewal but as he lived on the north side of Dublin, we only met infrequently at Charismatic Renewal conferences and sometimes at Full Gospel Business Mens' dinners. John went straight to the point. He told me two people had contacted him the previous evening. They were parents who had a problem. Their son, Stan was in hospital. He was stricken down suddenly with a disease, which apparently is so rare that it only strikes about one child in a million. John went on to explain that while the disease could be diagnosed, no treatment to combat it had yet been found by the medical profession. John pronounced the name of the disease which I could neither repeat nor spell; nor had I ever heard of it previously. The parents of the sick child knew of John's involvement in Charismatic Renewal and urgently sought any assistance he could offer. As it was late at night when the parents were in touch with John, he said he would think about the matter and promised to contact them as soon as possible. While shaving that morning, John continued, my name suddenly came to his mind, hence his telephone call. I anticipated what was coming next. 'Andy,' he said, 'will you come with me to visit Stan?'

I stalled. I had no desire other than to protect my 'holy hour' on television from 4.30 pm to 6.30pm (a Kerry joke?) that afternoon. To get myself off the hook I asked John would the parents have any objection to me visiting their son. I was trying to buy time. John replied as quick as a flash, 'Andy, you sound as if you would prefer to speak to the parents yourself?'

I agreed.

He concluded by saying, 'Thanks, Andy, I'll arrange it.' We put down the phones and I hoped that they would not contact me until later that same evening at the very earliest.

But my friend John did not exactly hang about as within minutes I received another telephone call. It was from the sick child's father. He introduced himself and said he had just been on the telephone to our mutual friend, John. 'Andy, my son is very ill. I should be so pleased if you would visit him,' he said.

'When would you like me to see him?' I asked, hoping that he might ask when it would suit me.

'Could you ever see him today?' he asked, adding that both himself and his wife were desperately worried over their child. 'John and I could pick you up at 4.30 pm at your office and the three of us could drive to the hospital and maybe avoid the peak traffic hour.'

The caller had indicated the only time when I wished to be free – my magic hour of 4.30 pm! At that moment it was just as well that he could not see my face. I agreed, we put down the phone and I said to myself, 'Bang goes my beloved soccer match.'

For the next few hours or so, as far as my staff was concerned, I must have been a very grumpy boss indeed. And to crown it all, my second-in-command came in to see me in the early afternoon to ask could he leave the office early. He said his work was up to date and he wished to see the match on television. I wished him the best of luck!

At 4.30 pm precisely, my callers arrived, I was introduced to the sick child's father who thanked me for coming and we set off. So instead of hurrying home alone to watch a football match I found myself in the company of two men driving to a city hospital. But our attempt to avoid the peak hour traffic failed miserably as within minutes we found ourselves in a traffic jam in Grafton Street. There, the child's father said, 'My son is in great pain for the last three days, Andy.' His remark didn't register with me – somehow it passed over my head. So there and then with the car stationary, the three of us began gently praising the Lord for the healing of Stan. We progressed slowly through the traffic, arrived at our destination, parked the car and John and I followed the child's father into the hospital complex. As we hurried along one corridor, we suddenly heard shouts and screams and unerringly seemed to be heading towards the very location of that commotion. We entered a ward and there in the far right hand corner we saw Stan. He was screaming and shouting and immediatey he saw his father he wailed, 'Daddy, Daddy, take the pain away – take the pain away!' His father hurried to him and held him in his arms. But the pain which the little boy was suffering must have been frightful as he tossed from one end of the bed to the other, as if someone was literally throwing him around. All the while he continued screaming and shouting, pleading with his father to take the pain away. John and I stood there in shocked silence. It was only then I realised what the father of the child was endeavouring to convey to me when he told me in the car in Grafton Street that his son was in extreme pain. I couldn't visualise it then – now I could. The scene was so awful that both John and I were stuck to the floor. It was for us the beginning of a nightmare in reality.

To be suddenly confronted with such a stressful situation had the effect of almost totally immobilising me. Whatever about my friend John, I could neither think, talk or act. Then I began to hope that maybe the child was in a spasm of pain which would soon pass. But the minutes dragged on and when I eventually whispered my hope to John he slowly shook his head. 'Andy, he has been suffering constantly like this for the past three days,' he said. Only then did the full horror of the position dawn on me as the shrieking of the little boy continued unabated. I was so overcome that I could not look at the child but I did manage somehow to make a hurried sign of the cross on the back of Stan's hand as he was tossed around in pain. The little boy was turning almost cartwheels in the bed, endeavouring, it seemed to escape the pain as he screamed and shouted. I wondered how the father could possibly stand this seemingly endless stress.

There was a small table near the bed so John and I rested on it. 'John,' I said, 'put your hand on mind, on this table and we will ask the Lord to accept our hands on each other, as our hands on Stan.' John did so and there we were part of this dreadful scene. Having children of our own both of us could identify with the suffering which we were witnessing as father and son huddled and twisted together while we listened to the father trying to console the boy but to no effect. The tears just rolled down my face unashamedly. I remember praying or thinking, 'Lord, I'm not

able for this one. I am only an insurance man and John is a com-
munications man. Both of us are out of our depth here. Lord, we
haven't the background, training or conditioning which is part
and parcel of the make-up of doctors, nurses and para-medics
which enable them to professionally and objectively deal with situations like this one.' I presumed John was praying too but I was
much too confused to be aware of it. But through the tears and
the distress we managed somehow to praise the Lord for the healing of Stan. We prayed from Scripture, repeating the Lord's words
'Suffer little children to come unto Me' and 'Unless you become
as little children you cannot enter the Kingdom.' But all the time
the terrible din continued. I recall saying, probably out loud,
'Lord, I don't know what my friend John had planned for this
late afternoon but I had planned to be very far from a place like
this, looking at football.' And I reminded the Lord that there were
thousands of people looking at this match while we were here. I
acknowledged to the Lord that John and I were not better or holier
than these people but at that moment we were different in that
we were specifically praising His name. In desperation I even
repeated St Theresa's prayer which she was known to use when
under extreme stress, 'Lord, if this is the way you treat your
friends, it is no wonder you have so few of them.' Then the
two of us, half sitting on that table, said the Lord's prayer but we
were so emotionally affected that neither of us could even attempt
to read Scripture. We prayed in tongues but could hardly hear
ourselves with Stan's continuous screaming. How John and I
endured this turmoil for an hour or more I will never know.
Several times I was tempted to just run away as the tormented
boy kept wailing, crying and shouting. On and on it went and
there seemed to be no end to it.

But we continued to pray all during that time, because I suppose there was nothing else we could do. I remember almost
abusing the Lord as six o'clock passed, wondering if this nightmare
would ever go away: 'Lord, on this lovely summer's evening, there
are people playing golf, playing tennis, sailing, swimming, eating,
drinking and even looking at television – but Lord, we are here.
We are Christ's men, however sinful and unworthy, trying to
minister in your name to this little child by just being here. Lord,
there is nothing we can do and apparently there is nothing the
doctors can do either. But Lord, you can heal him.' Then after

enduring this terrible din and confusion for so long, John and I had one of the most astonishing experiences of our lives. The noise which was so constantly overpowering and stressful then suddenly ceased but astonishingly we were not conscious of the ensuing silence for almost a minute. So when it eventually dawned on me that Stan had stopped screaming I became very fearful. In the healing ministry I had now come to accept that one must always be conscious of death. Slowly I said, 'John, look at Stan and see if he is dead of alive.'

John looked across me and as I watched I saw his face, amazingly transformed from shock to joyful disbelief. 'Look at him, Andy, look at him!' Slowly I turned my head and there I saw Stan spread out all over the bed, silent but totally alert. There he was in his Dad's embracing arms, peeping out with his beautiful brown eyes at the two men half-sitting on a table, one with his face in a mess with tears. In sheer astonishment I realised that there was no sign of pain in his eyes or face. On the evening of the third day, the pain had left him, the screaming had ceased.

At that moment a fourth man joined us, an uncle of little Stan. In some amazement the newcomer asked 'How are you Stan?' Stan replied in a very composed tone of voice. 'I'm very well, Uncle Dick.'

'Would you like something to eat, Stan?' his uncle asked.

'I'd love chips, Uncle Dick,' Stan replied.

Uncle Dick dashed out of the ward and within minutes was back with a bag of steaming chips. Stan's father arranged his son the right way up in the bed and smoothed the coverings as his boy began to devour the chips. A nurse passed by, then stopped, turned around and said somewhat incredulously, 'You are eating Stan!' Apparently he had not eaten anything for days.

'Is there any vinegar in this place?' Stan asked the nurse who was standing stock still looking at him. The nurse took off even faster than Uncle Dick and returned with the vinegar which Stan proceeded to lash on to the chips. All the while John and I were like shell-shocked troops as we surveyed the totally changed scene. Stan's father at last stood up from his son's bedside chair, turned and put his arms around us. The three of us just stood there together. None of us could speak even one word. At last Stan's Dad said, 'John will drive you back to the office, Andy. Thanks for coming. There is no way I am leaving now.' We made our farewells and left the ward, little Stan being much too busy with his chips to even notice us.

We walked down the hospital corridor, slowly but still joyfully shocked. John was first to speak. 'Andy, I have heard of instant healing when people praise the Lord but to see one has just blown my mind.' I was simply unable to speak. I do recall John driving me to my office and I seem to remember us trying to sing the song of praise 'He is Lord' but we didn't make a good job of it. John left me at my car park and said, 'Andy, what a wonderful day we have had.' We hugged each other with joy and he drove away.

I went straight to my favourite restaurant and decided to celebrate. It was Wednesday evening when I normally have a meal in town. I said to the waiter, 'I'll have a very special steak.'

'Yes, sir,' he replied. 'You look like someone who made a killing at the office today, sir.'

'Yes,' I said, 'I had a good day today, Praise the Lord,' and with a beautiful meal I celebrated Stan's recovery. When I had finished I asked the waiter, 'Who won the match today?'

'What match?' he asked.

Well you can't win them all, I thought.

A week later I met Stan's father who confirmed the good news that his son had recovered. One could read the sheer thankfulness on the man's face.

But similar happenings witnessed by other people were to continue, as I went out, by invitation, to visit the sick.

'WHAT IS HAPPENING TO MY HANDS?'

Mark is a very successful business man whose career went in several directions. After the minimum of schooling, he joined the army where he enjoyed a carefree life for four years. In civvy street he had a variety of jobs but was always drawn to the selling end of things. He went from one salesman's job to another and even worked for two multinational companies. Eventually he went into business on his own and once said to me, 'Andy, having my own show on the road has given me the greatest job satisfaction.' But everything must be paid for, even in this life and Mark knows only too well the meaning of business pressures. He realises (and so do I) how true the old saying is 'If you can't stand the heat, then what are you doing in the kitchen?'

However our story starts on Spy Wednesday afternoon when the business heat was cooling off – for both of us. Mark had made an appointment with me and picked me up at my office at around 4.30 pm (a familiar time for these happenings) on the Wednesday of that Holy Week. We were bound for a city hospital to visit a friend of his. Easter was here again and both of us were glad to be getting away from business for a few days.

So a familiar scene was repeating itself – two men in a car crossing Dublin city, to visit the sick, while praising the Lord *en route*. Mark outlined to me how he had prepared for the visit. He left his factory in the early afternoon, went into town, had been to Confession, Mass and Holy Communion, after which he came straight to my office. He wanted his friend healed when we laid hands on her in the name of the Lord and he had prepared as well as he knew how, to give our mission every chance.

Mark was in the Renewal but how he came to it I never knew. He was another Dublin northsider and as such I only met him infrequently. Having negotiated the city traffic while praising God, we drove into the car park of the hospital. Before leaving the car we praised the Lord. I recall saying, 'Lord, both of us bear two names very familiar to you when you walked this earth – Mark and Andrew. We know from Scripture that when you first sent out your seventy disciples, you sent them out two by two. They returned and reported that they had witnessed the blind see, the lame walk and cripples being made whole when they laid hands on the sick in your name. Lord, the two of us are going out in your name also. Grant that we also may see what your first disciples saw.' We said the Lord's Prayer and left the car.

Entering a ward we met Mark's sick friend, Margaret. It was a four-bed ward. But Margaret was so embarrassed at the sight of two men actually coming to pray with her for healing that she immediately requested us to draw all the drapes surrounding her bed! We did so and there we were, the three of us, completely cut off from everybody in the ward. Margaret had never heard of the Renewal and knew nothing of the healing ministry, so I told her we were prepared to pray with her to the Lord to seek her total healing. I stretched out my hands towards her and said, 'Here are my hands, Margaret. Should you be willing to place your hands in mine, we will begin. But may I say, we don't push, sell or force this particular approach to the Lord. So should you have any reservations or even the slightest objection to our way, well that will be the end of the matter and certainly we will take no offence.' Margaret looked at Mark first, for a few seconds, next at me and then very slowly placed her hands in ours, saying, 'Oh, please do pray for my healing.'

I never discussed Margaret's medical condition with Mark but it was evident that she was crippled with rheumatism of some sort. Her hands were in a semi-clenched position and in no way could she open them or straighten any of her fingers. Mark and I held them very gently in case our touch might cause her pain and distress. Because Margaret was so insistant on the immediate drawing of the drapes when we arrived at her bedside we now found ourselves without chairs. So I sat on the bed at Margaret's left side while Mark knelt on the floor at her other side and we began praising the Lord. I thought what an extraordinary sight – a lady in a hospital bed with one man sitting on the bed, another kneeling at her bedside and all three holding hands praising God!

On the bedside locker I had laid out what I now referred to as my healing kit, composed of my scripture and the holy oil. This oil was given to me by a nun who was also active in the healing ministry. She informed me that it was oil blessed by a bishop on a Holy Thursday for use in the presence of the sick. The good nun steeped cotton wool in the oil and placed the very moist wool in a container to prevent the oil spilling and staining the contents of my briefcase. This oil is, I think, referred to as the oil of gladness by people in the Renewal. So each of us made the sign of the cross on ourselves and on each other with this oil after which we read Psalm 37 from Scripture. It is so comforting and consoling to tell a sick person that the Psalms were prayers used by the Lord himself during his time on earth. Maybe he even said Psalm 37 on one of his journeys' to Jerusalem. Next Mark and I prayed in tongues. The three of us said the Lord's Prayer, Hail Mary and Gloria and so concluded our healing effort.

We gently released Margaret's hands, Mark stood up while I reached over to the locker to gather up my kit. Our visit had lasted approximately three-quarters of an hour and so I said, 'There it is, Margaret. We came in the Lord's name, you graciously accepted us, we laid hands on you, praised the Lord, prayed in tongues, sent forth His Word, prayed spontaneously, said the Lord's Prayer and blessed each other with the oil of gladness. There is nothing more we can do. But acknowledging that the power to heal resides in the Lord we must accept that the timing of the healing must be His alone.' Margaret had just laid back on her bed rest but now seemed to be studying her hands intensely. Suddenly her left hand began to open slowly, the fingers and thumb straightening. Margaret, totally astonished, cried out, 'Mark, what is happening to my hand?' Then the right hand began to open in a similar manner and she began to shout, 'Look at my hands! Look at my hands!' I was sure that the sound of her voice could now be heard in the corridor outside the ward. The embarrassment which she felt on our arrival had now well and truly disappeared. Then she sat bolt upright in the bed, began turning, twisting and rubbing her hands together, and staring at them like someone who had just found a pair of hands. Looking at them in complete bewilderment she cried out, 'The pain is gone, Mark, the pain is gone!'

Mark could neither move nor speak. I asked were her hands painful before our visit and she replied, 'Oh, my husband touched my elbow last night and I screamed with pain.'

But the excitement was not over yet. Margaret, now very elated, blurted out 'What is happening to my legs?'

'I don't know Margaret – you tell us,' I said.

'My legs are moving! My legs are moving! I can move my legs!' she cried out, and she began to plough the bed with her legs. She then reached out both arms and joyfully hugged us as we thanked the Lord. We pulled back the drapes, Margaret began to call out to the other women in the ward, telling them the good news and as a nurse appeared we left.

Mark seemed to be in a state of shocked silence (I know I definitely was) as we walked down a corridor making for the hospital exit.

'Wait here, Andy, while I make a phone call,' he said.

He returned within minutes and said, 'You are having your evening meal in our house.'

I protested saying, 'Mark, the deal was that you would return me to my office. It is most unfair for you to land me in on your wife unannounced and expect her to include me in the family meal.'

'I have just phoned her and you will be as welcome as the flowers in May,' he replied. 'You will have to tell the family what we have witnessed with our own eyes just now – they would never believe me!'

And so we travelled on to Howth where I met his lovely wife and family and was entertained to a beautiful meal. The excitement of seeing the events in the hospital ward and describing the happening to Mark's family was no good at all to my digestive system. But when Mark recovered his composure and began to talk I settled in and enjoyed the lovely meal. When I declined the wine at the table, the hostess seemed to be somewhat relieved. Up to that moment she must have been wondering whether or not the two of us were sober! The eldest boy of the family who joined us later at the meal was a medical student in his last year at college. He listened very intently to our story and simply observed that it would be a good yarn to tell the lads at college on the following morning!

On our return journey from Howth, Mark and I reviewed joyfully the extraordinary events we were witnessing in the Renewal. We promised to meet again after Easter but when we did so to go on a healing mission the wrong person was healed!

A VANISHING ACT

On a Friday afternoon I was walking back to my office after lunch as the seemingly endless traffic flowed in two lanes down Lower Leeson Street heading for Dublin's city centre when I heard a voice calling my name. I looked in the general direction of the call and there I saw my friend Mark, driving in slowly moving traffic.

'Can you spare a few minutes?' he shouted.

'I'm sure I can,' I answered. He immediately stopped the car, opened the passenger door and said, 'Jump in.' I did so and then he explained that his daughter was in a nearby hospital. 'We will visit her and I will have you back in your office in a few minutes. I checked with the Burlington Hotel but was told that you had just left. I am glad to have found you so easily.' He went on to tell me that his daughter had been admitted to hospital for tests, the nature of which he did not disclose. We arrived at the hospital and went to his daughter's ward but to Mark's surprise, he found her bed empty. On making enquiries, the word was that she had been sent to another hospital for tests and was not expected to return until late that afternoon.

Mark being a very positive man was not going to waste a chance of a healing opportunity. He found two chairs, put them at the side of the empty bed and said, 'Come on, Andy, we will pray that everything will be all right with my daughter, although we cannot physically lay our hands on her.' So we sat down and prayed together for a few moments. A middle-aged ward sister passed, stopped in her tracks and looked at us. We must have presented an unusual sight – two men with bowed heads beside an empty hospital bed! She approached us and asked, 'Are you all right?' which was a good question in the circumstances. We stood up and explained our position. The sister seemed to understand, turned away to continue her walk down the ward but suddenly stopped, came over to me and looking at my left eye in a very professional manner enquired, 'What is that on your eye?' There was a small cyst on my lower left eyelid, so I said, 'It looks like a hard cyst but it is neither sore nor painful.' She continued her question asking how long had it been there, while all the time examining my eye.

'I suppose it is there some weeks now,' I replied.

She then said very authoritatively, 'Wait here.'

Off she went and returned within minutes with a small phial of ointment. She came very close to me, examined my eye again and said, 'Put this ointment on your eye, morning and night for a week. If that cyst is still there, then come in here and we will whip it off.' Then in a very quiet and confident voice she said, 'Close your eyes.' I did so and with the thumb of her right hand she made the sign of the cross on my left eye, saying gently, 'In the name of the Father and of the Son and of the Holy Spirit.' I thanked her and she left us.

Mark and I quit the hospital and he drove me back to my office, promising to keep in touch. Entering the office I went immediately to the cloakroom to have a good look at my eye. There in one of the large mirrors I examined it but there was no trace of the cyst on my left eye – it had simply vanished! My first reaction was that I was examining the wrong eye, so I checked the other eye, but there was no sign of a cyst there either. Again I examined my left lower eyelid very closely and slowly but could not find any cyst nor was there a mark on the eyelid where the cyst had been. Thoroughly perplexed, I returned to my office to continue my afternoon's work. My secretary, Siobhán came into my office about an hour later with correspondence to be signed and remarked, 'I see, Mr O'Neill, you got the cyst removed from your eye.'

'I was in hospital at lunch time,' I replied, truthfully enough.

'I noticed that cyst on your eye for the past few weeks. It is always prudent to have these things attended to in the early stages, to avoid bother later,' she continued, and leaving the correspondence on my desk departed. I hadn't the sheer nerve to tell her how it all happened.

I took the phial of ointment out of my pocket, stood it on the desk and proceeded to check and sign my correspondence in the usual way. At the end of the working day, I pocketed the ointment, returned to the cloakroom and again checked my left eye. It was still clear. I drove home, bewildered and when I entered the house, my wife began serving the evening meal. I sat down and put the phial of ointment on the table.

'What is that for?' Delia enquired. So I explained how I unexpectedly met my friend Mark and described our visit to the hospital.

I paused but before I could continue Delia said, 'I see you got the cyst removed from your eye.'

'The cyst is gone – that's for sure,' I replied, and then I outlined the action of the ward sister. Delia stopped serving the dinner for a few moments, said nothing and then continued with her task. When we were both seated at the table, Delia asked, 'Were you joking about the ward sister and your eye?'

'I wasn't,' I replied and I again explained in detail the events in the hospital and my two visits to the cloakroom in my office. The astonishment which I experienced in the cloakroom that afternoon was still with me. There we left the matter.

At home on that Friday night I must have checked my eye in the bathroom mirror some half a dozen times before retiring but the cyst had completely disappeared. I went through the same routine of checking my eye next morning but again found it clear.

I expected Mark to contact me during the following week concerning his daughter and I was looking forward to telling him of my remarkable experience. Apparently Mark knew the ward sister whom we met and I planned to thank her on our return there. But Mark did not contact me, which did not surprise me, knowing the business pressure under which he operated. So I telephoned the hospital and described the ward sister (whose name I did not know) to the receptionist there and was lucky enough to locate her. I told her my story and thanked her. The ward sister listened very respectfully and said how glad she was to hear the good news of the cyst's disappearance and she told me that she invariably made the sign of the cross on every patient, at first examination. But further than that she would not expand. Maybe Christian healing experiences were not so infrequent after all.

I learned later that Mark's daughter was discharged from hospital some days after our visit, all her tests being negative.

However, the happenings, experiences or healings – call them what you will – were to continue as this two-by-two phase progressed. But first the urge to undertake a deeper study of the Renewal, which desire had been with me for some time now, had to be fulfilled.

6

Teaching an Old Dog New Tricks?

The current Trades Apprenticeship Training scheme in Ireland incorporates an off-the-job training period. In this scheme an apprentice in the first year of his chosen trade is sponsored by an employer. The employer pays the wages of the apprentice while he undergoes a year's training in a state training school. He then returns to his employer and is accepted as a second year apprentice. At this stage of my progress in the Charismatic Renewal Movement it occurred to me that I should begin a close study of it, on lines similar to the off-the-job apprenticeship training scheme, in the hope that it would compliment the on the job training which I had already experienced. Basically this proposed study was an endeavour on my part to mature, a striving to achieve some theoretical or academic knowledge of this world-wide Renewal.

A cursory examination of the prayer meeting scene universally, reveals that there are many different types of prayer meetings, each displaying its own peculiar action. One can find evidence of shared prayer meetings, totally silent meditative or contemplative prayer meetings, prayer meetings whose object is to encourage devotion to particular saints, prayer meetings whose aim is to promote a certain Christian way of life, Marian prayer meetings and so on. But at a very early stage in my studies it became apparent that there were several basic, fundamental, definite, indispensable elements, easily identifiable in a classic orthodox Charismatic Renewal prayer meeting.

So I decided to base my study on close personal observation of the action which I both saw and heard at the weekly prayer meeting which I attended in Avila, Dublin, and also by observing other prayer meetings where possible. The first of these elements which I found in my prayer meeting was the praising of God, which was both specific and two-fold. Audible words were used, such as 'Praise God, Praise the Lord. We bless the Lord. We thank you

Lord. We praise the Father, Son and Holy Spirit. We bless you Lord for your Church which is the Body of your Son Jesus Christ. We thank you Lord for just being here. We praise and bless you Lord for your goodness, kindness and mercy. We thank you Lord for giving us your Son. We bless you Lord for sending us your Spirit with His power' – and so on.

This spontaneous praising of God in words was extended to include songs of praise accompanied by the music of guitars, flutes, recorders, tambourines, and the like, all combining to produce joyful sounds. In all this activity and sound I discerned that many people had acquired a new uninhibited freedom in prayer. It was probably, I detected, a joining together of like minds by people who were confronting their Creator personally, a bursting forth of sounds springing from the primitive desire of human beings to reach out, contact and praise their God. There was also evidence of symbolic prayer with the raising and clapping of hands. Even dignified shouts of praise could be heard. It appeared then that many people had, in effect, experienced what is beautifully termed as the 'eighteen inch drop' – from the head to the heart, in the praising of God at Charismatic Renewal prayer meetings. One of the side effects of this joyful out-pouring of praise was that many of the participants were filled with a peace and a joy which was plainly obvious.

The second easily identifiable element in a Charismatic Renewal prayer meeting following the praising of God was the manifestation of tongues. Tongues is as old as the apostolic age but is in our day a new way of saying *Alleluia*. At prayer meetings, this praising of God in tongues begins when many people spontaneously join together in a speaking tone of voice, then it gently develops into a plain chant-like sound, all of which seems to bring calmness and peace to the participants. Immediately the tongues cease, invariably there is a deep silence as the tradition has grown that tongues promote yet another gift of the Spirit – prophecy.

With this third element, prophecy, it is evident that people gathered together at a prayer meeting acknowledge that here they enter into deep spiritual mystery. In the silence following the tongues, one person would normally be led to prophecy and maybe that prophecy would be followed by another or even a third. Prophecies which I can recall were more or less on the following lines:

My, people, I have put my praise on your lips.
Bring my praise into every situation of your lives
And I will show you the power of my praise,
      says the Lord!
My, people, turn away from evil,
Come to me
Be in the world but not of it,
Honour my Son and
I will give you peace and contentment,
      Says the Lord.
Even should a woman forget the child she bore,
I will not forget you
Your name is written on the palm of my hand,
      says the Lord.
Give me your sick and I will heal them
Your worries and I will dispel them
Your burdens and I will carry them
My people, I want to set you free,
      says the Lord.

Apparently all down the ages the Lord always spoke to his people through his prophets and in a Charismatic Renewal prayer meeting, these people of God (*populi Dei* as Pope John XXIII called them) in this our age, also wait on the Lord in silence, seeking to hear his word spoken to them in prophecy. Listening to prophecies at a prayer meeting can be a deeply peaceful spiritual experience.

The fourth element was readily discoverable, as leaders of prayer meetings insist, week-in and week-out, that the foundation on which the Charismatic Renewal movement is built, is Scripture. Short Scripture readings are part and parcel of the action at prayer meetings. These readings are always received in respectful silence by people who believe that the Lord is speaking to them when his word is sent forth at their meetings. I reflected that this attitude is wholly in the spirit of Vatican II, which endeavoured to restore Scripture to its rightful place in the lives of Roman Catholics. As regards these Scripture readings, I acknowledge that I grew up in a Catholic tradition which concentrated on the Mass, the Sacramental system and devotion to Mary and the various saints. But the indispensable place of Scripture in the life of a Christian was only discovered by me when I became exposed to the Renewal.

Praying the Scripture was never part of my Catholic tradition and I could not help remembering that my first healing experience occurred when a man, rigid with fear and tension, totally relaxed in my hands at the very moment when I prayed the Scriptures.

The fifth element which came to light in my study of prayer meetings is called teaching. As the meeting draws to a close, the leader calls on a person to deliver a prepared paper on some aspect of the Christian faith. This teaching is usually a ten minute affair. The most popular teaching themes appear to be based on explanation of some parts of Scripture or some conclusions which can be drawn from Gospel parables or from healings by the Lord during his life on earth. As academically qualified Scripture scholars are very thin on the ground in Ireland, authentic deep Scripture commentaries are very hard to come by in the Renewal and as a result many prayer groups are unable to provide a scholarly Scripture teaching service.

The sixth element apparent in a prayer meeting is testimony. This particular element has no definite time slot so it may surface at any time. Many people are led to witness to the things which they say the Lord is doing in their lives. The subject matter of these testimonies is as wide and as varied as life itself. Again these testimonies are listened to in silence, may or may not be of general interest and at times are greeted with applause. It must be appreciated, though, that people who gather at prayer meetings are not drawn from any definable class or type. Prayer meeting doors are open to all comers, saints and sinners alike and some wag once remarked that those who gather at prayer meetings are not checked for either sanctity or sanity! But it is clearly evident during the giving of testimonies that people in the Renewal are not embarrassed in publicly witnessing what the Lord is doing in their lives and have acquired a new mature freedom of expression in their daily struggle to live out their lives in accordance with Christian principles. But allowances must be made when some testimonies are unclear or may be, exaggerated.

The seventh and last element of a Charismatic Renewal prayer meeting as I see it and the one on which the meeting usually ends is concerned solely with prayer of petition. During this period many people seek the assistance of the assembled group, in their quest to the Lord for favours. Christian people all down the ages have constantly and with hope sought divine intervention in their affairs. This prayer of petition is based solidly on Scripture and is rich in Christian tradition. It is an experience which is both gentle and consoling to listen to people individually outlining the things which trouble them as they seek assistance from the Lord in matters of sickness, unemployment, personal relationships, spiritual, domestic, social, business, financial or marital difficulties. During this time also people who in previous weeks have made prayers of petition, outline favours received. Such items of good news are invariably greeted with joyful applause. But every facet of human life is liable to be heard during this part of the prayer meeting. Maybe these many and varied caring aspirations demonstrate why so many people can identify with and relate to the whole Charismatic Renewal experience.

From this general study then, I drew two conclusions:-
(1) that a classical orthodox Charismatic Renewal prayer meeting must manifest seven basic indispensable elements, namely, the praising of God in words and in songs of praise, tongues, prophecy, Scripture, teaching, testimony and prayers of petition; and
(2) its members must be open to the power of the Holy Spirit and must confidently expect to see the gifts of the Spirit made manifest in their own lives.

I have witnessed these seven elements constantly at the 'Avila' prayer meeting and the regular testimonies of its members confirm that the gifts of the Holy Spirit with signs and wonders are truly evident in their lives.

The theory of any subject is normally acquired by study, by attending seminars and lectures and by discussion with people interested and involved in it. But it seemed to me that the healing ministry, being only so recently renewed in Catholic circles in Ireland, was almost totally lacking in text books. Books like Katherine Kulman's *I Believe in Miracles* and Francis McNutt's *Healing* and *The Power to Heal* appeared to be the only serious studies on Christian healing readily available to me. Seminars at weekends and at National and Regional Charismatic Renewal Conferences in Ireland on Christian healing are practically non-existent. So to match my on the job training with theory, I was left with only one avenue – to discuss Christian healing with people engaged in it and such people are hard to find, believe me.

In such discussions as I could organise and promote the use of tongues was often examined and repeatedly I heard it advocated that when one is in the presence of the unknown, the use of tongues is of fundamental importance. The realm of the unknown which often confronts me in the healing ministry is confined to two areas – alcoholism and drug abuse.

With alcoholism I had an extraordinary relationship. I am a life long teetotaller but I do not make this claim boastfully, a complete disinterestness in alcohol being the reason for this life-style rather than any strength of character. I did my stint in sports which were closely associated with massive drinking sessions when victory (or defeat!) celebrations were called for. I spent many hours in the company of pint drinking companions during raucous sing-songs but, while I sang with the best of them, the whole drink scene was a total non-event for me. It was strange, then, that with such a background I should have been instrumental in assisting people who had serious drink problems, to establish not alone one but two branches of Alcoholics Anonymous. Whatever organisational expertise I possessed was apparently useful to, and availed of, by these people. But when these two branches of AA were set up and going, I moved out, making an odd appearance at their open meetings again in a consultative administrative capacity during their formative months. When people with serious drink problems sought assistance from me in the healing ministry, my first instinct was to point them in the direction of AA, an organisation for which I have an extremely high regard. But sometimes it is not prudent or feasible to offer such advice to these people on initial contact.

The second area of the unknown to me is drug abuse. Of this evil I know very little and unlike alcoholism, a general agency like AA is now only beginning to surface in Ireland.

Now it is generally accepted that tongues is one of the most common gifts of the Holy Spirit which is made manifest at Charismatic Renewal prayer meetings. St Paul refers to tongues as the least of the gifts. It is as well to emphasise that the Charismatic Renewal Movement of the Holy Spirit is not concerned with teaching old dogs new tricks. Rather is it an endeavour to restore all things as they were in the infant Church in the days of the first Pentecost. Tongues are as old as the first Pentecost and are referred to in the Gospels, in the Acts of the Apostles and in the Letters of St Paul.

In endeavouring to understand in some way or to describe

tongues I am often reminded of a friend of mine who is a professional gambler. It is indeed facinating for me to listen to him as he describes his attitude to gambling at race tracks. The ordinary punter goes to the races seeking winners but when my friend goes racing his first task is to seek to know the horses who are not expected to win! So in a nine-horse race if he can reasonably establish that six of the horses are not fancied by their connections or by the odds on offer, then his task in seeking a winner is substantially reduced. The real field for him is confined to three horses. Similiarly it may be easier to indicate what tongues are not, when we approach the task of endeavouring to define this phenomenon.

When people use tongues they are not wishing evil, telling lies, announcing doom and gloom, boasting, swearing, taking the Lord's name in vain or damning people with faint praise. But to compile an exhaustive list of the sins of the tongue is not my objective here but simply to stress that praying in tongues is a positive thing. Continuing to tease out the mystery of tongues by defining what it is not, it can be readily appreciated that the discipline of words is unnecessary when one uses tongues, thereby affording one a new unrestricted form of expression which can be a real fulfilling positive spiritual experience.

I remember well discussing tongues with friends in the Renewal when one chap remarked, 'I could never pray in tongues – it just wouldn't be me.' Whereupon someone immediately replied, 'You could be right, Jack – it could be the Holy Spirit!'

But little by little, step by torturous step I was accumulating some theoretical knowledge of tongues which is such a necessary support when those in the healing ministry are confronted with the mysteries of alcoholism and drug abuse. This introduction to an academic knowledge and understanding of tongues was to grow and expand and when faced by alcoholism or drug abuse in people seeking release from the bondage of these afflictions, I became more and more convinced that the use of tongues was of paramount importance in the ultimate rehabilitation of these suffering human beings.

HEALING

After my attempt to study the Charismatic Renewal Movement generally and acknowledging that I was involved in healing, it seemed a natural progression to proceed to a clinical examination of the healing ministry, which is promoted and encouraged at its prayer meetings. It also seemed logical that to begin this study I should have some knowledge of the history, tradition and development of Christian healing and I approached this task in the spirit of an off-the-job training exercise.

It is generally accepted now that in the last decade or so, the Charismatic Renewal movement has largely restored world-wide the age-old Christian custom of the laying on of hands on the sick seeking their recovery. This approach is so new to many Catholics in our day that it is necessary to stress that the laying on of hands to heal is not a matter of teaching an old dog new tricks, rather it is a striving to return to Christian tradition and roots, an attempt to restore all things in Christ as in the building of the infant Church in the days of Pentecost.

In the public ministry of Christ the Jews witnessed many instant healings. Healings were not unknown to the Jews all down the centuries of their history but the sheer scope, constancy and power of the healings by Jesus had never been remotely experienced in human history. Nothing could withstand his healing power which was in no way selective. All kinds of illnesses and diseases were instantly cured by his touch as were afflictions of the mind. Evil spirits in people young and old were readily identified by him and cast out. He even raised the dead to life.

Reading the accounts of the public life of Jesus in the Gospel we find that he preached and he healed. When he sent out his disciples, one of his specific instructions to them was to heal the sick. Scripture scholars inform us that twenty per cent of the Gospels are devoted to his healings. We find the Gospels, Acts of the Apostles and Letters of the New Testament strewn with accounts of healings by Jesus and by his apostles and disciples in his name. For instance in the Gospel of Matthew we find them in chapters four, nine, ten and twelve. In Mark we find them in chapters one, six and twelve, in Luke in chapters six, nine, and ten and in John in chapters two, four, five, six, nine, and eleven. We find healing advocated powerfully in the Letter of St James. Healing is part and parcel of the Acts. We may read of them in Acts chapters three, five, six, eight, nine, fourteen, nineteen and twenty. Now these Scriptural references can be gleaned from mere cursory examination of the Gospels, Acts and Letters and are in no way exhaustive or indicative of deep scriptural study on my part. Suffice it to say that healing was a fundamental element of the message of Jesus, a manifestation of his total power over all things and the way he chose to bring the good news to so many broken people. So it is plainly evident that when Christians accept Jesus, they must accept him with his healing power. If one can make allowance for the terminology Jesus Christ is a complete package deal for Christians!

To my mind the one fundamental message which each of the four Gospels spells out is that, above and beyond everything else, Jesus Christ came on earth principally to found a Church. So in this light it is interesting to take a quick look at the tradition of healing in His Church. We learn something of the healing ministry from the writings of the Fathers of the Church. For instance St Ireaneus in the second century wrote that some of his community were engaged in healing the sick by the laying on of hands in the name of the Lord. We have the same message in the fifth century from St Augustine. But Augustine is an interesting study in the healing context in that he had to be converted to accept the power of healing in the name of Jesus. Apparently he once held that the gift of healing was confined to the apostolic age. But the Holy Spirit had a surprise in store for him when he was installed as Bishop of Hippo. In those days in that cathedral adult baptisms were the order of the day and when the newly baptised men and women, all clad in white to celebrate the occasion, emerged from Augustine's cathedral, into the brilliant North African sunshine, their friends and relatives gathered round to congratulate them with hugs, kisses and handshakes. To their surprise many sick people, on touching the newly baptised, found themselves instantly cured of illnesses and diseases of all kinds. So a healing tradition grew up there and Augustine invariably saw a queue of sick people outside his cathedral on adult baptism days. He further witnessed personally many of the sick being instantly cured when touched by the newly baptised. So Augustine acknowledged his error and accepted graciously that healings in the name of Jesus by the power of the Holy Spirit were as valid in his day as they were in Apostolic age.

But then it appears that the widespread tradition and practice of healing the sick by the laying on of hands by Christians seemed to decline universally. I once remember a nursing sister saying to me that the Church then lost its healing ministry but I know that this is not so. The healing ministry declined but did not disappear from the life of the Church. Rather it seemed to become confined to shrines and special places of worship, to certain people whose personal holiness and sancity were acknowledged in their own life times and to places to pilgrimage. A priest friend of mine and a celebrated Scripture scholar, discussing the accepted decline in the healing ministry of the church, came up with the explanation that at certain times the Holy Spirit puts away the healing ministry in safe places! But he asserted that the Church by its very nature could never lose its healing ministry and had always maintained it in one form or another. It may well be that this decline in the laying on of hands tradition was also partly due to the rise in the knowledge and practice of medical and surgical skills.

I know that although I mixed in Catholic organisations and movements all my life and kept myself fairly well informed on current Catholic thought and teaching I can honestly say that the Christian tradition of healing was totally unknown to me until I became exposed to the Renewal. Nor did the healing ministry appear to be emphasised in the sacramental system of the Catholic Church either. Even one of the sacraments was almost misnamed being referred to as the Last Sacrament. When one heard of the family of a sick person sending for a priest then it could be safely assumed that the undertaker would follow closely behind! Nowadays this sacrament is more correctly named as the Sacrament of the Sick, a channel of grace which can be used to obtain healing of mind, body and spirit as well as preparing the sick for death and judgment. So the Renewal has spilled over even to renew the liturgy of the Church.

I was then immensely consoled to realise that the healing ministry was not kinky or a way-out cult but was solidly based on Scripture, Christian tradition, the writings of the Fathers of the Church and was, and always will be, an integral part of the faith of Christians.

It is also interesting to note that the healing ministry seems to be playing a role in the striving for unity by the various Christian churches. In the last decade or so since the emergence of the Renewal there has been a unique coming together of the three great Christian traditions – the Catholic Church with its sacramental system, the Protestant Church with its insistance on the promotion of the Word of God (Scripture) and the Pentecostal Church with its emphasis on the power of the Holy Spirit – manifesting itself in largely attended world-wide Charismatic Renewal conferences and prayer meetings at which the healing ministry is accepted, studied, promoted and practised. The healing ministry, then, could well be one of the foundation stones on which the eventual unity of the Christian Church may be built.

It is generally held that the Church with its divine and human nature will always need reform and it may well be that the healing ministry is playing another important role in modern days in the renewal of the Church and its Christian community. Sadly many people nowadays publicly declare their rejection of the Christian faith into which they were born and casually announce their irreligion, atheism and paganism. Such people, I find, when confronted with healings by the power of the Holy Spirit are confused, silenced and astonished. Apparently total concentration and insistance on having the fun in life by people who reject the Christian faith denies them all ability to assist others in any way. Signs and wonders are far removed from hedonistic life styles. Unfortunately the logical end of many atheists when the going becomes too tough in their lives is suicide.

So from my study, discussion, deliberations and reading, prompted by the Charismatic Renewal Movement and its healing ministry, it would appear that the Holy Spirit has not removed healings from shrines, places of worship, relics, holy people dead or alive, pilgrimages or novenas, but wishes Christians in this day and age, to be as bold as Peter and John when they cured the cripple outside the beautiful gate of the Temple. Now, Christians, living ordinary lives, are finding a new boldness which was not formerly part of their make up and are no longer afraid or embarrassed to seek health in its widest forms for themselves and others by the power of the Holy Spirit in the healing ministry.

So having assimilated a little academic and theoretical knowledge of the Charismatic Renewal Movement and its healing ministry it was, I thought, time for me to return to where the action was and to again make part of my free time available to the sick seeking healing by the power of the Holy Spirit.

7

Signs and Wonders?

One Thursday in August I decided to treat myself to an outing in the fresh air after my day's work, so I arranged a game of golf that evening. But Paul, a friend of mine and a member of the 'Avila' prayer group, rang on that morning, seeking to set up an immediate appointment with me. Paul, who is also active in the healing ministry, wished me to accompany him on a visit to a lady who was ill and in great pain. Hearing of my previous engagement, he at once volunteered to collect me at my house the moment I arrived home from work that afternoon, drive to the sick lady's house where we would spend half an hour in prayer with her seeking healing and then return to my house, leaving me ample time to fulfil my golf commitment. When I agreed the arrangements I reflected that hustlers were not confined to the insurance industry!

Paul arrived at my house dead on time and we headed for the home of the sick lady on that beautiful summer's afternoon and during the short drive he unfolded her medical case history. Some days previously she has contracted shingles on her lower back and thighs and sought medical assistance. But despite the doctor's best efforts she had endured frightful pain during the previous three days and nights. The sick lady, who was a member of our prayer group, was a widow who lived alone. We arrived at her house, parked the car but before alighting shared a prayer. We reminded the Lord that we bore two names, Paul and Andrew, which were very familiar to him when he walked this earth, were going out in his name, asked that our visit be blessed by the power of his Holy Spirit and boldly expressed our desire to witness the healing power of the Spirit that afternoon as his disciples did in the days of the first Pentecost. We said the Lord's prayer, left the car and knocked at the lady's door.

After some minutes the door was opened and Sheila welcomed us. She looked very ill indeed. All normal colour had left her face, her speech was very faint, she could barely walk, was trembling all over and looked utterly weary. Slowly we entered the sitting room with her and pulled three chairs together. Sheila outlined the history of her illness and said the pain was so severe the previous night that she cried out several times for the Lord to take her. There was no way, she avowed, that she wished to continue living, should the pain persist. Her doctor who had called that morning gave her pain killing tablets but sadly expressed the opinion that the pain would persist for the next six weeks or so. Unfortunately the pain killers did not work so Sheila was in a very bad way indeed at the time of our visit. She told us that the neighbours, who knew of her condition, very kindly checked her position regularly. So Paul, Sheila and I held hands and praised the Lord for her healing. We read some short passages from Scripture, prayed in tongues, recited the Lord's prayer and then made the sign of the cross on ourselves and on each other with the holy oil.

We were in action for some fifteen minutes or so when an astonishing transformation came over Sheila. Before our very eyes, Paul and I first saw the colour flooding back into Sheila's face, then her voice was restored to its normal tone and finally her trembling ceased. With a look of total surprise on her face Sheila announced to us very calmly and confidently that the pain of the shingles on her body was decreasing rapidly. So we renewed our prayers as fervently as we could for some minutes and then Sheila, as cool as a breeze, said, 'I am completely healed.' So we blessed the Lord for His power and mercy, Sheila escorted us to the door, thanked us profusely, and we left.

So in amazement we returned to my home where Paul dropped me. His face was aglow and I am sure mine was too. I entered my car and headed for my golf appointment, singing in tongues all the way.

On Friday, the day following our visit to Sheila, before my evening meal, I went to the Forty Foot in Dalkey for a swim. It was another glorious evening and the sea there was high, clean and calm. What more could a fellow desire?

Coming away after a most enjoyable swim, I met a friend of mine, Jim, about to go swimming. He called me and asked, 'What did Paul and yourself do with Sheila last night?' Unknown to me, Jim was a neighbour of Sheila's. Small world! So I told him of our visit and described the happening in Sheila's home. Jim then said, 'I called to see her last night after you two left and to my surprise found her completely normal. I contacted her again this morning and found that she had enjoyed a deep untroubled night's sleep.' Sheila also confirmed to him that the rash of the shingles and the pain had disappeared and during the night she did not use a single pain killer either. With eight hours uninterrupted sleep, she didn't need to. The shock on Jim's face was lovely to see. So we praised the Lord for his power, while standing at the edge of the Forty Foot and I left my friend with a very puzzled look on his face.

The following Sunday evening Sheila rang me and said she was having a Bridge party at her house that evening and was doing the catering herself for her seven visitors. On that Sunday the scene in Sheila's house was radically changed from what it had been on the previous Thursday. How different the situation was now, I reflected, when the power of the praising of God was released into it. Apparently four days is a long time in the healing ministry.

AN UNUSUAL INSURANCE CLIENT
AND A UNIQUE EXPERIENCE

I received a telephone call in my office on a Wednesday afternoon. It was unusual in that it came from a nun. She had an insurance problem. On the recent death of her father, who was a widower living alone, she found insurance policies issued by my firm among his possessions. The nun wished to ascertain their value and began informing me of the details of the policies which were before her on her desk. I made some rough notes as she continued to read out the particulars of the policies. After a while it became evident to me that both of us were getting nowhere in this telephone exercise, which could go on for a long time, because of my caller's unfamiliarity with the policy format. So I suggested that I should arrange a call to her convent by one of my inspectors who could visually examine the policies and other relative documents and then explain the whole position to her in a matter of minutes. She gladly accepted my proposition and we at once proceeded to arrange a mutually acceptable date. Then it occurred to me that it was a Wednesday afternoon and maybe I could make the call myself. I enquired as to where her convent was and it proved to be only a very short distance from the Burlington Hotel where I normally went on Wednesday evenings for my pre-prayer meeting meal. So I suggested that I could call to her shortly after five o'clock on that same afternoon and she agreed.

So after my days work in the office I found myself knocking at a convent door. I was ushered inside and was led to a small reception room to await Sister Maura who had telephoned me. Sister Maura arrived carrying a folder, we greeted each other and sat down at a table. She produced the policies and other documents and I went to work on them. I assessed their current value, instructed her to forward them to her solicitor while I promised to confirm their value to him as he would need the information for the preparation of the necessary Schedule of Assets for probate purposes. The whole operation took some twenty minutes or so. We stood up, the nun thanked me for my visit and I replied by saying, 'It is good to have the whole matter tidied up so quickly, Praise the Lord.' The good Sister suddenly looked very startled and exclaimed, 'Did you say Praise the Lord?'

'I did,' I replied.

Then with a look of total surprise she said, 'Don't tell me you are in Charismatic Renewal?' When I pleaded guilty she said slowly, 'Sit down – tell me all about it – you hardly look the type!' The good sister asked for it, didn't she!

So I spent a few minutes telling her how my life style had changed with the coming of the Renewal. She listened very attentively and then just said, 'Will you pray with me?' and slowly reached out her hands across the table.

'Pray with you for what?' I enquired.

'For just about everything,' she answered. So there we were in a convent, a nun and an insurance man, holding hands across a table with our heads down, praising the Lord. What a way to end an insurance call, I reflected. But I was very wrong – the call wasn't to end just then. Sister Maura seemed very consoled by the prayers which lasted some five minutes or so and said to me with her face flushed with excitement, 'Could you wait just a moment – I would love you to meet Sister Joan,' and with that she scampered out the door and left me alone. I wondered just what was happening.

Within a few minutes there was a knock at the door and my new friend returned with Sister Joan who said, somewhat incredulously, 'I believe Mr O'Neill you pray with people.' Hearing such a remark from a total stranger in a convent before six o'clock on a Wednesday afternoon, simply shocked me as I wondered where this Renewal business was taking me. So the three of us held hands and praised the Lord for all our needs, again for a few minutes. That did it. Sister Joan said to her companion, 'We must go and get Sister Dympna!' and off the two of them fled before I could move from the chair. I was sure now that my visit was getting more ridiculous by the minute. But on it went. Sister Dympna came in alone, introduced herself and said very gently, 'Thank you very much for offering to pray with me.' Her words shook me. I came to that convent on an insurance query and here I was praising God with the nuns! It now appeared that the nuns in that convent were queued up outside the door of the reception room in which I was seated! This scene of the nuns coming to me and praising the Lord and going out to send in other sisters was repeated many times until Sister Maura finally reappeared with yet another nun and introduced her as Mother Superior. As if I was not confused and bewildered enough already, Mother Superior said to me, with a twinkle in her eye, 'Mr O'Neill you seem to be disrupting the life of our convent this afternoon.' I was at a complete loss for words which is unusual for me. 'Sister Maura informed me that you called here on your way home to your tea. I apologise should we have delayed you,' she continued. I recovered my speech and told the good lady that I did not return to my home on Wednesday evenings as I normally dined in the nearby Burlington Hotel prior to attending a prayer meeting. Mother Superior immediately responded, 'Would you care to join us for tea and maybe tell us about the Renewal?' Before I had time to say a word I found myself being shepherded along a corridor and into a very bright and attractive dining room. It appeared that hustlers were everywhere in my life and that the Renewal was certainly leading me into strange places, I reflected.

So there I sat with Mother Superior, Sister Maura and two other sisters, at tea, with the remainder of the community at other tables in the dining room. It was a wonderfully relaxed occasion for me as we discussed the Renewal. It is common experience that when people gather to speak of the Lord, His word and prayer meetings, time flies. So before I realised it, an hour flew by and tea ended. Mother Superior then said to me, 'Mr O'Neill, would you be so kind as to lead the community in a short prayer meeting in the Charismatic Renewal manner?' When I replied that I would be very honoured to do so, all the dining tables were pushed back, the chairs were arranged in a circle, we sat down and began to praise the Lord. Looking round at the scene and realising that it was all totally unplanned amazed me. We read from Scripture, praised the Lord in words and sang a song of praise to him. Then after some ten minutes or so, having decided that I had done my share, I prepared to end our little prayer meeting. Before I could do so, a telephone rang nearby, a nun went to answer it, returned quickly to Mother Superior who immediately left the room. I decided that when she returned I would make my farewell. Mother Superior was not long delayed on the telephone and quickly rejoined us. As I thanked her for having me – and for my tea – she said she wished to make and important announcement to her community. For some three years, she informed the gathering, the community in that convent had been under a considerable strain concerning a certain matter, the nature of which she did not disclose to me. Apparently it became necessary to seek legal assistance but the matter would not go away. A settlement could not be reached and the position continued to worsen and the stress on the community increased month by month. Mother Superior then revealed that the telephone call which she had just received had come from their solicitor. He informed her that, out of the blue, the other parties to the dispute came into his office unannounced that afternoon and when discussions finished at around seven o'clock the whole matter had been settled – sealed, signed and delivered, to the satisfaction of all parties concerned. Mother Superior very formally concluded, 'I wish to praise and thank the Lord for lifting this burden from us after all these years during this prayer meeting.' Her announcement was greeted with delight and applause and after handshakes and hugs all round I left a joyful community.

That Wednesday evening I had certainly shared a unique experience with the community and the look of joyful shock and surprise on Sister Maura's face as she saw me to the door said it all.

So the happenings and healings progressed from a convent to a hotel where people whom I had met in business were to experience both the power of the praising of God and healing.

THERE IS NO SUCH THING AS A FREE LUNCH

Part of my managerial responsibilities is concerned with providing clients with mortgage finance for the purchase of private dwellings. This operation brings me into constant touch with builders, auctioneers and solicitors. So a telephone call which I received one morning from a managing director of a building and construction firm, was not unusual. As it transpired, his firm was about to erect a scheme of private dwellings and realising that the vast majority of the potential purchasers would be seeking mortgage finance, my caller wished to have all the available information on the current mortgage scene. In plain language he wished to pick my brains and he was welcome. Both of us had a mutual interest – people buying houses brought very acceptable business to my firm.

So I explained the main outlines of our mortgage finance arrangements and indicated that his firm would be responsible for providing certain documentation, such as plans of the properties, site plans, specification, copies of planning permission, certificates of earnings, certificates of reasonable value and building contracts. I presumed my caller was taking notes as I spoke but then he came up with a proposition. 'I would like to meet you to discuss the matter further. Could you meet me for lunch some day this week?' he enquired. Having consulted our diaries we agreed to meet at a hotel on the following Wednesday.

On the morning of the lunch date, the managing director's secretary rang to ask would it be possible for me to call to his office (which is just a short distance from where I work) at around 12.30 pm that day. Such an arrangement would obviate the need for him to drive to my office and so, hopefully, we would avoid being snarled up in peak lunch time traffic. I agreed and so at precisely 12.30 pm on that day I presented myself at the spacious reception centre of the construction firm. I was expected and was asked to take a seat. Opposite where I was sitting, a young very attractive girl was standing facing the exit. I next noticed a car pulling up outside. The driver, a lady, alighted from the car, walked round to the other side of it, opened the passenger door, left it so and returned to her seat. A uniformed doorman in the reception area then walked slowly to the exit door, held it open and nodded to the girl. The girl then took off like a deer, ran out the door, positively leaped into the passenger seat and slammed the car door behind her. The car then drove slowly away. I was so completely engrossed in this extraordinary scene that I did not realise my builder friend had been standing for some time beside me. I stood up, he greeted me, we went to his car and drove to the hotel.

Surprisingly for me, we there met the builder's wife who was joining us for lunch. I reflected, however, that as my host was paying the piper he had every right to determine the company. But I soon learned that the wife was an active working partner in the building firm, finance being her special responsibility, hence her presence at the lunch. During a very enjoyable meal I outlined in some detail the terms and conditions of my firm's mortgage finance scheme and again indicated the necessary documentation which would need to be supplied by their firm. The wife took extensive notes during the meal and also asked many questions. There was no doubting that I was in the presence of a pair of very hard working business people. Eventually she closed her notebook, both my hosts thanked me for my assistance and we all visibly relaxed. I realised that I had worked quite hard during the meal and recalled the old saying that there is no such thing as a free lunch. Everything which one receives in this life must be paid for – one way or another.

As we prepared to leave the table the managing director mentioned to his wife that I had witnessed Angela's exit act from the office. At this remark she asked us to remain seated for a while and disclosed that Angela was her secretary. Angela and herself worked very closely together and my host's wife went on to say that Angela was a very capable, efficient and dedicated worker: But unfortunately Angela was an agoraphobia sufferer, which explained her abnormal behaviour in leaving the reception area on that day. She then went on to describe Angela's lifestyle. For years Angela had not been out and about and was restricted to life in her home and office. She had to be driven to and from work. Attendance at any outdoor sporting event was impossible for her nor could she go to the mountains, countryside or seaside. Since her school days she had to view all these places from the inside of a car. She could only attend church or theatre provided a car was available and it would need to be driven as close as possible to the entrance of any building which she wished to enter. Even at home on summer weekends Angela could neither walk or sit in the garden. All she could do was to stand at the door and look out at the garden and at the beautiful sunshine. Constant and extensive medical treatment had failed to bring any improvement in Angela's condition. She brought Angela's story to a conclusion by saying, 'I would love to do something to help her.' In an effort to conclude the lunch, I again attempted to leave the table, remarking that I was in the Charismatic Renewal movement and its healing ministry and maybe Angela might be interested to hear of it sometime. Unfortunately, my remark delayed me another half hour. Both my new friends wished to hear so much of the Renewal and its healing ministry that I had extreme difficulty in breaking off the engagement and getting back to my office. But the managing director's wife looked like someone who had just discovered something important. She was even more alert and interested listening to the signs and wonders of the healing ministry than when recording the bits and pieces of mortgage finance. As we parted she promised to be in touch with me concerning Angela and the Renewal.

I hadn't long to wait for her to contact me. She rang the following morning and explained that she was in a telephone kiosk outside her office. This was real cloak-and-dagger stuff! She enquired as to where I usually had lunch. On learning that I frequented the Burlington Hotel, she thanked me and promised to be in touch again.

The following morning she was on the line again from the public telephone call box. A trap was about to be laid for poor Angela! She went on to explain that she had discussed the Charismatic Renewal and its healing ministry with Angela on the afternoon of our lunch date. Obviously an action woman who didn't hang about, she now disclosed that she wished to bring Angela into my company in a very relaxed and leisurely way, just for starters. So the great plan was unfolded to me. The scene was to be set in the Burlington Hotel the following day. My instructions were that after lunch I was to stroll from the restaurant through the lobby where I would find herself and Angela having coffee and sandwiches. I was to go over and join them (this business lady was obviously used to issuing precise instructions). I would then casually chat to them while sitting on the couch. After some minutes she would excuse herself from our company on the pretence of making a phone call and then I would have Angela all to myself for about ten minutes. The rest, it appeared, would then be up to me! I was asked, 'Andy, are you willing to have a go at laying hands on Angela for healing?' At that moment I was conscious that I was developing a rare talent for attracting hustlers!

'Right – we will see where the Lord leads us,' I replied.

'I'm really excited over this "get together" – a thousand thanks,' she said.

At lunch in the Burlington Hotel the following day I felt more like a secret service agent than an insurance man. Then with my meal finished I set out in the best James Bond manner and as per instructions strolled through the hotel lobby. There on a settee I spied my co-conspiritor with Angela whom I immediately recognised, saying, 'Fancy meeting you here.' I greeted her and was introduced to Angela. I sat down with them and the scene was set. Having chatted for some minutes the director's wife made her pre-arranged departure and headed for the telephone area in the lobby. I didn't beat about the bush with Angela. Straight away I informed her that I was in the healing ministry of the Charismatic Renewal Movement. She was immediately interested. I told her the story of a recent healing which I had experienced when I had laid hands on a person. Then without more ado I said, 'Angela, all of us need healing, every day. Should you ever desire to praise the Lord with me for any healing which you might desire, I would be delighted to be of assistance.'

'I would love to do so but it would hardly be possible here,' she responded. Angela was sitting to my left, so I said, 'Should you wish, you can place your right hand on the settee beside me. I'll then touch your hand and praise the Lord for your healing.' The word agoraphobia was never mentioned. Angela placed her right hand, palm downwards on the settee, I covered it gently with my left hand saying, 'I am asking our heavenly Father through His only begotten Son Jesus Christ, by the power of the Holy Spirit, to heal you. Praised be Jesus Christ, Amen.' At that moment the director's wife re-joined us, I bade them farewell and went back to work.

Some days later I had yet another phone call from a very excited lady. She exclaimed, 'I'm phoning from the public kiosk again. At lunch time today Angela left the office by herself and walked around the block! She returned and told us that she proposed to do it again tomorrow and would even endeavour to cross the road, too! Isn't it wonderful news, Andy,' she concluded. So both of us praised the Lord for His power and His mercy.

Angela's agoraphobia days were over. I met her some six weeks later and she looked radiant.

'How's life, Angela?' I asked.

'I'm taking driving lessons – I'm buying a car next month,' she replied and off she sailed down Dublin's Leeson Street, skirt swinging, scarf waving and fair hair flowing, looking as beautiful and as majestic as a merchant ship of olden days, at sea, under full sail. Apparently the Burlington Hotel had been the scene of yet another happening. Interestingly enough, in the months following this incident, my mortgage finance business developed and multiplied in an astonishing manner.

SIGNS ON A SATURDAY

On a beautiful spring Saturday Joe, Paul and I found ourselves driving into the spacious grounds of a convent, some twenty miles from Dublin's city centre. A non-residential retreat was being held there for some one hundred and fifty members of Charismatic Renewal prayer groups in the area. Having been heavily and constantly canvassed over a long period by the retreat organisers, we eventually agreed to join their panel of speakers. The retreat began with a prayer meeting on the Friday night followed by two full day sessions on the Saturday and the Sunday. According to the programme my talk was slotted in to the Saturday morning session, while Paul was to speak in the afternoon. So we decided to spend Saturday at the convent, while Joe came along to be available to pray with people. Following my talk, the organisers had planned a healing session and the three of us were included in a healing team of six people. This team was split up into three pairs who were available to minister to people in the period from the end of my talk until lunch.

After lunch there was a session of prayer and praise led by a music group which was followed by a talk given by my friend Paul. At the conclusion of Paul's talk the retreat participants were formed into buzz groups, each group consisting of eight people. Six of the people in my group had only recently become involved in the Renewal, so when the discussion began they wished to hear of, and explore the phenomenon of, tongues. So we had a wide ranging discussion on this topic and at its conclusion I invited the newcomers to participate in an experiment which might lead to them being released in tongues. The experiment was based on the assumption that God helps those who help themselves! They agreed, so I encouraged them to endeavour to make sounds which were not words, letters or numbers. Neither were they to utter any words of any foreign language, nor indeed words in Irish! While they attempted to do so, the remaining person in the group prayed gently in tongues with me. Then very quickly it all began to happen. One lady was suddenly released in tongues and much to her astonishment began to praise the Lord in this manner. Next a man on my left received the gift. So it went on until all eight of us were praising the Lord in tongues. At this stage I encouraged the group to put their new gift to music – to sing in tongues – and then a wonderful surge of music was heard all over the hall. Word of what was happening in our group went round, resulting in people from other groups, who were ending their discussions anyway, gathering and standing around our group. The excitement mounted as those around us who had tongues joined in. Next the music group added to the joyful noise by strumming guitars, making haphazard notes on wind instruments and on the piano. The people who were newly released in tongues then left their chairs in our group, the chairs were immediately filled by others seeking tongues so I began the whole process all over again.

The wonder and the joy of it all was infectious. The next thing I remember was Paul placing his hand on my shoulder and saying, 'There are two angels here who want to get into the scrum,' and with that he pushed two gorgeous little girls, aged about five years, into the centre of the group. I gathered both of them in my arms and looking all round in wonder at this extraordinary scene, the tiny girls began effortlessly to sing in tongues. These innocent beings, I thought, having no inhibitions and being so utterly unaware of group dynamics, auto-suggestion, group therapy and the like, just sang naturally in tongues and enjoyed being part of this joyful scene.

It was difficult to disperse this rugby-scrum-like gathering but eventually it scattered with those newly-released in tongues being congratulated by their friends while the hall was being prepared for evening Mass. The mother of one of the little girls who was in our gathering came and asked me to lay hands on her daughter who had, she explained, a bad stammer. So for the second time in the afternoon I gathered that little girl in my arms and sat her on my knee. I said to her, 'Open your mouth darling.' She did so. I then said, 'Put out your tongue.' She obeyed and I quickly touched her tongue with the index finger of my right hand. At once I realised that I had said these words to the child and touched her tongue involuntarily. I had never done anything like it before. It all just seemed to happen. Then I asked the little girl to tell me her name. Her mother answered saying, 'Patricia McLoughlin.' Looking directly at the little girl I said, 'Patricia, I want you to repeat these words after me, "Jesus Christ loves Patricia McLoughlin".' The child repeated the words without hesitation or trace of a stammer. Next I asked her to repeat after me, 'Patricia McLoughlin loves Jesus Christ.' Again she did so, speaking in the normal manner like any ordinary child. I kept on looking at her and asked her to repeat over and over again, 'Praise God, Praise the Lord.' She did so without any speech stoppage whatsoever. I hugged Patricia who snuggled in to me and I returned her to her radiant mother, as Mass had begun. I was so overcome by this happening that I was quite unable to make the responses to the priest until Mass was well underway.

But the healings had not ceased. During the bidding prayers at Mass, a lady stood up and announcing her name, told the following story: 'The condition of my right arm is well known to the members of my prayer group. For six months now, I was unable to raise it above the level of my shoulders. Any attempt on my part to do so, would result in excruciating pain. Despite having constant medical attention with drugs, injections and physiotherapy, the condition persisted. However after Andy's talk on healing this morning, Joe and his companion layed their hands on my right arm, praised the Lord and asked for healing. When they took their hands away, Joe quietly asked me to try to raise my arm and extend it fully upwards. I did so and experienced no pain or inconvenience whatsoever.'

Her sharing was greeted with joyful applause. She concluded by saying, 'It is wonderful to know that I will by combing my hair myself in the morning,' and with that she waved her right arm in the air, extending it fully upwards.

With the healing of the child's stammer and a hand restored to full movement without pain, yet again healing had followed the praising of God by people at a Charismatic Renewal prayer gathering.

'WHAT IS GOING ON IN AVILA?'

I do not know how long the weekly Charismatic Renewal meeting
is in existence in 'Avila', Dublin, but I do know that it was alive,
well and swinging when I discovered it sometime in 1978. 'Avila'
is a monastery where Carmelite monks reside and, as is generally
known, the main work of their order is to teach prayer. So I
suppose it would be natural to expect to find a unit of the Charismatic Renewal movement in 'Avila', given that the Renewal is a
world-wide prayer movement. The Carmelites have occupied this
monastery since 1884 and all down the years, prayer, the divine
office and the Breaking of the Bread has continued there. It may
well be that all this unbroken spiritual activity is one of the reasons
why so many people experience a deep sense of peace on visiting
'Avila'. Many people openly testify and confirm this blessing of
peace experience on coming to the Charismatic Renewal prayer
meeting there. Given the history and tradition of the location,
perhaps then, this phenomenon is not all that strange.

Part and parcel of the prayer meeting in 'Avila' is the prayer
ministry which is exercised after every meeting, when the prayer
leader for the night invariably invites anyone who desires to be
prayed with, for any intention whatsoever, to proceed to the
oratory where the Blessed Sacrament is reserved. There a prayer
team of six to eight people gather and minister in pairs, to people
individually, who come there. After some years attending this
prayer meeting I was invited to join the prayer team. The whole
scene in the oratory is one of peace, whispered prayer of petition,
(and sometimes of thanksgiving) and quiet movement, as each
pair in the prayer team lay their hands and praise the Lord with
people individually, who form a ring holding hands, all in the
spirit of hope, calmness, love and intercession.

At this prayer meeting session one evening, two of us in the
prayer team met a middle-aged lady. She disclosed that she was
an asthma sufferer for years and requested prayers for healing. So
we held hands together and praised the Lord for a few moments.
The lady expressed her thanks and quietly left the oratory while
we proceeded to the next person. On the following Wednesday
evening at the prayer meeting, the lady who was the asthma sufferer, gave her name as Mary and testified that the moment we
touched her at the prayer ministry session, one week previously,

she immediately felt that the asthma had left her. Continuing her testimony Mary stated that she drove home after the prayers, went to bed and for the first time in years found that she could lie down in a prone position. She did not need to prop herself up with pillows in a sitting position wrapped in blankets. Nor had she to make any of her normal trips to her open bedroom window during the night. She concluded by saying that her inhaler was unused since the previous Wednesday for the first time in years and praised and blessed the Lord for the wonderful gift of deep untroubled sleep for the past seven nights, an experience which she had almost totally forgotten. Mary's testimony was greeted with applause.

At the conclusion of the meeting Mary came to me while most of the assembled gathering shared tea and biscuits and introduced her husband. With a look of complete shock on his face he said, 'Are you one of the men who laid hands on my wife last week!' I pleaded guilty straightaway! Then the three of us put our hands together and joyously thanked the Lord. Mary confided that when she came to the oratory for healing on the previous Wednesday, she did so with more hope than confidence.*

Apparently I had entered yet another phase in the healing ministry as the happenings were now to continue constantly at the 'Avila' prayer meeting.

'MADAM, I AM NOT IN THE PRAYING BUSINESS'

One morning in my office I received a telephone call from a lady. My secretary who put through the call announced the lady's name and address. The caller thanked me for receiving the call. She went on to tell me that she had four children, one married and three teenagers and was herself happily married. Wondering why I was the recipient of all this useless information, I continued to listen patiently to discover the nature of her enquiry. I did not rush her – in my business the customer is always right. When I eventually enquired as to how I could assist her she replied that it was a non-insurance matter. Hearing this I at once reminded her that I was a busy chap. Only then did my caller come to the point. She explained that she had seen me at the 'Avila' prayer meeting and would appreciate my assistance as a member of the

* This incident happened in 1981. Mary keeps in constant touch with the prayer meeting. The asthma has not returned.

healing ministry there. It transpired that her mother was ill and
the object of the call was to endeavour to arrange for me to visit
the sick lady. Hearing this, my first reaction was to try to back
off, pleading pressure of work but my caller at once came up with
a proposition. She explained that her mother's residence was close
to my office and offered to pick me up in her car at lunch time,
drive me to her mother's home where the three of us could have
a light lunch and then she could return me to my office, all within
an hour. Then the vital sales pitch came. She suggested, 'We could
do it all this afternoon should you not have a previous lunch date!'
The old saying about a free lunch came to my mind again. After
some hesitation, I said very slowly, 'Well, all right.' She concluded
her call at once by saying, 'Right then, I'll be outside your office
at one o'clock.'

So at lunch that afternoon I found myself in the presence of
two gracious ladies, June and her mother. June's mother who lived
alone was house-bound for some time past and obviously enjoyed
our company. We spoke of the Charismatic Renewal phenomenon
and in particular of its healing ministry, and after the meal June
and I laid hands on the sick lady who appeared to be very consoled
with the whole idea and the entire prayer routine. At this stage
June revealed that she wished to share a personal healing experience which transpired to be the real reason for our lunch appointment.

It appeared that some months previously June became unwell
and consulted her family doctor. Having listened to the history,
symptoms and nature of the complaint, the doctor examined her
and immediately suggested a chest x-ray which was duly completed
some days later. On receiving the x-ray results the doctor thought
it advisable to refer June to a specialist. The specialist investigated
her complaint and initiated a fresh series of tests and x-rays, the
results of which were all positive unfortunately. He sent for his
patient and told her that both lungs appeared to be affected. June
was shattered – the news was that she could have cancer.

Continuing her story in the presence of her mother and myself,
June said that at this stage she thought of the prayer meeting in
'Avila' of which she had heard some time previously. While she
had never been to it, she was aware that sick people were prayed
over there. So one Wednesday evening she arrived at 'Avila' to
her very first prayer meeting, alone and fairly scared. At the con-

clusion of the meeting she accepted the leader's invitation to proceed to the oratory for prayer. June explained that two ladies there prayed with her for a few minutes after she had informed them that she was unwell. June did not reveal the nature of her illness nor her fears. Having been prayed with June headed home, slightly confused at the sound and sight of her first prayer meeting plus the personal experience of the laying on of hands for healing.

The following week, June's specialist contacted her and a second series of tests and x-rays were conducted apparently to confirm the first diagnosis. This time to the surprise of the specialist, all the tests were negative and all x-rays clear. Being a prudent man he informed June's family doctor only, and decided to leave everything alone for a few weeks. Eventually the specialist again sent for his patient and his third series of tests and x-rays were completed. When the results were available, all proved negative and clear. So the specialist interviewed his patient and reviewed his findings with the three series of tests and x-rays laid out on his desk. Enquiring as to her general health, June informed him that she had never felt so well in her whole life, all symptoms and the condition which caused her to contact her family doctor initially having disappeared. The specialist, reviewing the whole position simply said, very slowly, 'Frankly, I'm puzzled here. The first results were definitely positive while the further tests were completely negative.' Breaking the ensuing silence, June somewhat timidly explained that having heard the positive results from his first investigation, she immediately attended a prayer meeting for healing. He replied, 'Madam, I am not in the praying business but I am in the medical profession and I find myself looking here at something which I cannot understand.' The specialist brought June's interview to an end by saying, 'Congratulations, you are no longer my patient.'

When June returned to her family doctor he revealed that he had been in touch with the specialist. Discussing with him the reason why the first series of his tests and x-rays were positive while the next two tests were negative, the family doctor suggested that some slight infection might have been present during the initial tests. The specialist totally rejected this suggestion intimating that what his first series of tests and x-rays disclosed could not be explained away in such a manner.*

* This happening occurred in 1980. June is still in splendid health.

So this was June's story, told to me in a very matter of fact way in the presence of her mother, whereupon we held hands and praised the Lord for His mercy and power. June returned me to my office and my head went down as my afternoon's work continued in the normal way after a very extraordinary lunch experience. In my way of making a living, business lunches are part and parcel of my scene, but on that particular day I had apparently partaken of a healing lunch. It was consoling for me to realise that this happening (or healing – call it what you will) was associated with the 'Avila' prayer meeting.

A PASSING PRAYER

After a prayer meeting in 'Avila' one Wednesday evening, I was enjoying tea and biscuits in the long corridor there, before proceeding to the oratory for the usual prayer ministry session, when I noticed Alice. The corridor was crowded and the level of animated conversation was noisily high. Alice, who regularly attends the meeting, brushed by me, gingerly carrying her cup of tea. I noticed that for sometime now she had been wearing a curvical collar. Apparently she had suffered a whip-lash injury in a car crash some months previously. We exchanged greetings and then she suddenly said, 'Andy for the love and honour of God, will you lay your hands on me to heal my neck!' I couldn't lay both hands on her as I had a cup of tea in one hand, so I placed my free hand on her neck and asked the Lord to heal it. Then as both of us were pushed in opposite directions by the crowd movement in the corridor, she said, 'Thanks, Andy,' and was gone.

The following Wednesday evening, coming towards the end of the prayer meeting Alice broke the silence which normally follows the singing in tongues and said, 'I would like a few moments to tell you my story. I attended the prayer meeting here last Wednesday and when it ended I joined my friends for tea in the corridor outside. There I met Andy and as he was passing I asked him to lay hands on me for the healing of my whip-lash injury. We hardly stopped moving while he did so. Mind you, I never had any belief or even the slightest interest in this healing and the laying-on-of-hands business and why I asked Andy to do it I will never know. However,' she went on, 'he did it and then I joined my friends for tea, a chat and a cigarette, before returning home.' She next outlined her normal morning routine after rising which included adjusting her curvical collar before coming downstairs to prepare the family breakfast. Then Alice declared that on the morning after that very quick laying on of hands, she arrived in her kitchen, prepared breakfast for the family and was working away at her house work for more than an hour, when she suddenly realised that she was not wearing her curvical collar. For the first time since her injury she had completely forgotten to wear it and astonishingly it only then dawned cn her that she had no need to wear it. So there and then she began moving, turning and stretching her neck in all directions without inconvenience or pain of any kind. To her total surprise, her neck was healed, for which she praised the Lord.

What staggered Alice was that previously she had no belief whatsoever in the healing ministry. At that moment, I thought, Alice could well identify with President Reagan who, on being upstaged by a political opponent, remarked, 'Well one cannot argue with success.'

A LADY IN DISTRESS

At the conclusion of the 'Avila' prayer meeting, Mary came to me. She was very upset indeed. Her car had been stolen from outside her flat the previous night, even with the steering lock on and a crook lock in position. She was very shocked when she opened her door that morning and found an empty space where her car should have been. She called into a police station on her way to work and reported the matter. She did not receive much consolation there as she was informed that dozens of cars were stolen every night in Dublin city. Mary asked me sadly, 'Andy, will you ever pray sometime that I will get my car back?' She was extremely worried concerning the possibility of her car being vandalised, even should she be fortunate enough to recover it. So telling Mary that there was no time like the present, we put our hands together and praised the Lord for the safe return of her car. For good measure we asked that the car be not damaged in any way. I remember well asking the Lord to have Mary's car returned to her in mint condition! This two-fold request to the Lord surprised Mary. Praising the Lord for the recovery of her car was fair enough but getting it back undamaged was a horse of a different colour.

But I could identify with Mary's distress. There she was, a young woman prepared to work hard for her living, with possibly her whole capital locked up in that car and suddenly it had been stolen. We finished praising the Lord and Mary left 'Avila' – to walk home.

At the meeting on the following week, I did not see Mary in the crowded hall when I arrived. But during the meeting, a lady gave testimony while remaining seated and I knew it was Mary. She simply said she wished to give thanks to the Lord for the safe return of her car which had been stolen. She did not outline the manner in which the car had been recovered but mentioned that she had been prayed with at the previous meeting, stressing how surprised she had been to hear the request to the Lord that the car be returned in mint condition. Mary concluded her testimony by saying that whoever stole the car must have washed it after it had served its purpose! The only loss was a small amount of petrol. The car was recovered totally undamaged.

After the meeting a very delighted Mary came to me, we held hands and praised and thanked the Lord for His goodness. Her joy was both overflowing and infectious as she left the meeting – to drive home! Truly, I reflected, as I too drove home that night, healing is as wide as life itself.

HEALING WITHOUT FUSS

As I parked my car outside 'Avila' on a lovely summer's evening, another car pulled up alongside me. A man alighted, we greeted each other and walked from the car park together. He informed me that some months previously he developed severe pains in both legs and after some time had to consult a doctor. He was extensively examined, tests were carried out and he was treated with various drugs and medicines. But the cause of the trouble defied medical identification and the pain remained intense, causing him many sleepness nights. He became so depressed that in time he ceased attending his doctor and reckoned that he would just have to live with the condition. Continuing his story, while we waited for the prayer meeting to begin, my friend explained that he had been attending at 'Avila' for some time before he decided one night to go to the oratory for the prayer ministry session. There he was welcomed by two girls and he informed them of the severe pain which he was experiencing in his legs. The girls, members of the prayer ministry team, hearing that the cause of his distress could not be medically identified, decided to pray in tongues for his healing. They did so and after all three of them had praised the Lord, he left the oratory and went home.

He went on to say that for some weeks after praying with the two girls in the oratory, in an extraordinary way he totally forgot the pain in his legs, until one Sunday afternoon while walking on Killiney strand, he suddenly realised how well he was feeling. The pain in his legs, which had been constantly present by day and night, was no more. Reviewing the previous weeks he was quite shocked to come to the conclusion that the pain had ceased from about the moment he attended the prayer ministry session in 'Avila'. He concluded that the gentleness of the healing ministry astonished him more than anything else. The pain seemed to have gone away without him even noticing.*

His story ended and yet another prayer meeting in 'Avila' commenced.

GIRL PROBLEMS

As usual another prayer meeting in 'Avila' ended with a round of applause for the Lord. People stood up, some to go home, others to head for a cup of tea or the prayer ministry session while more grouped together chatting away. This cheerful, joyful, bustling scene is always such a contrast to the peace, calmness and relaxation of a prayer meeting. In the midst of all this noisy chat and swirling movement of people, a lady came to me. She was the mother of a twenty year old daughter, who had problems. As the lady poured out her fears concerning her daughter's many and varied troubles and chatted away without interruption I was not sure whether these problems were of mind, body or spirit. But what I was sure of was, that this lady deeply loved her daughter. Her earnest care and concern that her daughter should get well was lovely to behold. I was experiencing once more a very beautiful thing – the love of a woman for her child. However, I did gather that despite regular medical attention for over a year, her daughter, Mary, was far from well.

My friend's dilemma was that Mary was not the prayer meeting type and her mother, Eileen, wished to bring her to 'Avila'. Eileen

* This healing happened in 1981 and the condition never recurred.

believed that healing is released by the power of the Holy Spirit when people publicly gathered to praise the Lord and she wanted that healing for her daughter. So Eileen came up with a proposition. She said, 'Andy, should I prevail on Mary to come here some night, immediately after the prayer meeting breaks up, I'll bring her to you. Will you please just lay your hands on her for healing there and then – and ask no questions! I want you to do just that – no more but no less.' I resisted the temptation to tell Eileen that I had enough troubles of my own without seeking to explore other people's problems but told her that I would try to do what she wished. So in the rugby-like scrum conditions which prevailed around us, I held Eileen's hands and asked the Lord to commence His healing in her daughter at that precise moment. I left her and headed for the prayer ministry session.

On the very next Wednesday evening, Eileen and her very scared looking daughter came to me immediately the prayer meeting ended. Eileen said, 'Andy, this is Mary,' and then she fled. So I found myself confronted with a very frightened girl. At that stage in her life, Mary was well aware that a little girl's life is not always sugar and spice and all things nice as the boys imagine. I held her hands – she was more or less a captive audience because of the jostling crowd around us – and said something like, 'Lord, bless this lovely girl. Heal her of anything which hurts her in mind, in body or spirit. And Lord, may I sing at her wedding!' I then kissed her in a fatherly way and I too, like her mother, fled and left Mary to find her own way through that crowded hall.

The following week Eileen and I met before the meeting began. As soon as I saw her I knew the news was good. She blurted out, 'Oh Andy, everything is all right! Everything has come right with Mary since the prayers last week. Everything – just everything is all right now!' So laughingly holding hands we thanked the Lord – for all sorts of everything! The healing which Mary received was known to herself, to her mother, and even to her boy friend! I did not need to know.*

* This happening occurred in 1983. Mary now regularly attends at 'Avila' and is flying!

8

Telephone Tapping

From 'Avila', the healing ministry with its signs and wonders dramatically branched out in an entirely unexpected direction. It all began with a casual remark which I overheard in the car park at the conclusion of a prayer meeting when one lady said to another, 'She rings me when she becomes depressed and I pray with her over the telephone.' Praying over the telephone? I had never heard of such a thing and in a million years would never have thought of it. If nothing else, these Charismatic Renewal people were very inventive, I thought.

Driving home that night I pondered on that casual remark – praying over the telephone. Only too well I realised that the telephone was absolutely necessary in my business life. The pair of telephones on my desk were in constant use. With their aid I could be in touch with clients, set up appointments, sell, motivate, be instantly available to my staff and head off trouble which constantly tended to arise in the very very competitive insurance world. My telephones, I appreciated, also brought their fair share of stress with which I had to cope, but everything has its compensations and a gratifying spin-off for me while on holidays abroad, is to hear telephones ringing in hotels and knowing that I will not have to answer them. Truly, holiday satisfaction means different things to different people. When I reached home that night, my thoughts concerning telephones, sparked off by a casual remark, ended and I never imagined even in the remotest way that a few words overheard in a car park were to affect me and many others in such a dramatic way. But like other aspects of the Renewal, events were about to overtake me and quickly proceeded from a casual remark to a casual acquaintance.

While on holidays in New York with my wife we met Mary in a hotel there. She was Irish, on a short business contract with her firm and returned home to Ireland on our flight. Mary enjoyed her six months stint working in America but was glad to be going home to take up her former post in Dublin. She was single and looked to be in her late thirties. Mary informed us on the flight home that she was about to have her own house built. She had been living in a flat in Dublin all her business life and had now decided it was time to have a permanent home, especially as there was no man in her life. Hearing I was an insurance man, Mary confided in us that she was absolutely ignorant of her insurance needs during the building of a house and also of her rights and obligations under a building contract. On a flight home after holidays the last thing in which I wished to become involved was a discussion on insurance. So to end the matter, I gave Mary my business telephone number and informed her that she was free to ring me the following week when I would take it from there. Mary thanked me, adding that there were many people in her firm who could assist but everyone of them seemed too busy to do so. After an in-flight meal, the aircraft lights were dimmed and I fell asleep.

However, some two weeks after our holiday ended, Mary contacted me as she urgently needed information and assistance concerning her house building project. So we decided to skip lunch the following day and meet in the Burlington Hotel for coffee, when I could give her a broad outline of the procedure. We did so and Mary found the meeting very satisfactory. We met there on two other occasions until Mary's solicitor took over. I was on call for Mary during the building of the house and when it was completed, I sold her an attractive with-profits endowment insurance policy, with the premiums helping to reduce her very high income tax payments. In this world, turn about is fair play.

Some six months after my last contact with Mary, she rang me from Monaghan on a Saturday morning. She was there visiting her father who was in hospital. Now everybody who meets me runs the risk of hearing of the Lord and Mary was no exception, being well aware of my connection with the Charismatic Renewal movement and its healing ministry. On the phone she informed me that her father was very ill and wondered would it be possible for me to visit him that day. As a request to travel from Dublin to Monaghan on a Saturday morning at a moments notice was, to say the least of it, unreasonable, I naturally had to decline the invitation.

Mary went on to tell me that her father was eighty years of age but added that no matter how old one's parents are, nobody likes to lose them. Then she cried. It was lovely to hear her expressing her love for her father through her tears. Mary then volunteered the information that her father had developed a very painful rash on his back and was literally in agony, needing nursing attention night and day. All medical efforts to heal it had failed. Suddenly I recalled the casual remark I had overheard some time previously concerning prayer over the telephone and realising that the patient was well beyond the three score and ten mark, I said to Mary, 'Would you be prepared to praise the Lord with me on the telephone for the healing of the rash which is troubling your father?'

Mary agreed and then very slowly and hesitantly, for the first time ever on the telephone, I found myself praising the Lord. I began by thanking him for Mary's father and his family. Then praising the Lord we brought that power into the whole situation and simply asked the good Lord to heal the rash which was causing so much pain to the patient and so much distress to his daughter. We finished by reciting the Lord's prayer, Hail Mary and Gloria. Mary thanked me and I returned to the garden where I had been mowing the grass.

After lunch I was sitting in a deck chair in the sun, reading the daily paper when the telephone rang. It was Mary again, ringing from Monaghan and she seemed very excited. She exclaimed, 'Andy I have wonderful news. After my call to you this morning, I left the hospital and had my lunch. When I returned I found that my father's rash had disappeared! It vanished during our telephone call!' I was so astonished that I could hardly speak. I just did not know what to say. But Mary went bubbling on, 'Oh, Andy, it is so lovely to see my father relaxed and calm, completely without pain. How wonderful it all is. Thanks so much, Andy,' she concluded and the call ended. I returned to my deck chair in the garden but did not pick up the newspaper. Was this happening a one-off affair or a mere coincidence, I wondered? But unknown to me a new chapter in the healing ministry had opened with Mary's telephone call on that Saturday morning.

THE GIFT OF BI-LOCATION

'Christmas comes but once a year and when it comes it brings good cheer' was a little ditty sung by a former generation. It was Christmas time again and yet another year in my business life was drawing to a close, with thankfully targets and growth percentages achieved. So with the business pressure tapering off, my attention was, as usual, focused on the completion of the annual accounts. As area manager, my responsibility was two-fold: to develop and promote my firm's business while at the same time maintaining efficient administration. Both went together like a horse and carriage. But somehow the pace of life seemed to quicken considerably during the last weeks before Christmas as office parties and staff dinners had to be fitted in to the normal routine.

On a Saturday evening some days before Christmas, the telephone rang in my home just as my wife and I were going to a party. It was a lady. She introduced herself and informed me that she was a member of a prayer group on the north side of Dublin. She too was about to leave her house but was heading for her prayer meeting. Her name was Peggy and she had a request to make. Unfortunately her husband, Bill, had suffered a stroke some weeks previously. It was a left-sided stroke, resulting in paralysis of his side, leg and arm. He was also unable to speak. Bill was in hospital. Peggy then asked me would I be so kind as to visit her husband and lay my hands on him for healing. It appeared that she had discussed her husband's illness at her prayer meeting the previous Saturday night, when a lady informed her that I was a member of the healing team in the 'Avila' prayer group, and maybe could assist. Realising that it would be impossible for me to fit in a call to a city hospital on the north side of Dublin, with the pressure of business and social commitments in the run-up to Christmas, I had to regretfully decline Peggy's request.

However, remembering the telephone call to Monaghan hospital and its dramatic result, I offered to praise the Lord with Peggy, there and then on the telephone, for the healing of her husband. Peggy was surprised at my offer, saying that she had never before heard of anyone praying on the telephone. So I explained that in no way was I forcing or selling this idea, but in the circumstances it was all I could offer. Peggy without any enthusiasm, commented, 'Well, I suppose it won't do any harm,' whereupon I asked her to repeat the words 'Praise the Lord', while I prayed. She did so and I praised the Lord for Bill and brought the power of the praising of God into his illness. I asked the Lord to lay his merciful healing hands on Bill, now that our hands were on the telephones. We concluded our prayers for Bill's healing by reciting the Lord's Prayer, the Hail Mary and the Gloria. I wished Peggy a happy Christmas. Delia and I then headed off to our party while Peggy, I presumed, went off to her prayer meeting.

The following Saturday evening at 7.30 pm my telephone rang. It was Peggy. She asked me did I remember her. Frankly, I didn't and I told her so, since, having praised the Lord for situations in peoples' lives, I immediately forget these circumstances and ask Him to bless all concerned in them so that these tragic events should not burden me in any way. But when Peggy reminded me that she had phoned me on the previous Saturday evening concerning the illness of her husband Bill who had suffered a stroke, I then instantly recalled our conversation. 'I have good news, Andy.'

'What is it?' I asked.

'Andy at the time of our prayers over the telephone last Saturday night, the stroke left my husband! He is home now and very well. His memory is not fully restored but the doctors assure me that it will come right in a matter of weeks,' she answered.

'Are you joking? I asked.

'No I am not, Andy,' Peggy replied and added that the nurses at the hospital had confirmed that the stroke left Bill at around 7.30 pm the previous Saturday night. She thanked me profusely for the prayers and said that Bill's healing was the best Christmas present which she could wish for. I asked Peggy to convey my congratulations to Bill, we thanked the Lord for his power and mercy, I again wished her a happy Christmas and our conversation ended.*

Having now experienced two instant healings when praising the Lord on the telephone, it would appear that the Holy Spirit was tapping the telephones, when two people praise the Lord in this manner! Then a mind blowing thought occurred to me – maybe the gift of bi-location was being made manifest in our day and

* This incident occurred in 1981. I know both their Christian names – Bill and Peggy – and the name of the hospital where I was invited to visit. I never knew their surnames, address or the venue of Peggy's prayer meeting. The only contact I ever had with Peggy was confined to the two phone calls described above.

age, when the people of God use modern methods of communication to praise Him?

My healing kit had, I reflected, consisted of my Scripture and the holy oil. Now, after Peggy's second call to me it appeared, that to this kit the Lord had added a third element – the telephone – which was both extraordinarly powerful and very convenient when used in His service, in the healing ministry.

'CHARISMATICS IN MY PARISH?'

The parish priest was concerned, puzzled and slightly confused. Some three months previously he had heard that some of his parishioners had formed a Charismatic Renewal prayer group. The venue of this prayer meeting rotated weekly in the homes of six or seven families involved. This prayer group, his curate lately informed him, was now attracting some twenty or more people, which the parish priest observed was no great cause for concern. But for the last week there was a buzz of excitement around his parish, generated by these Charismatics. It appeared that their normal house prayer meetings were to be suspended for seven weeks as all the participants had signed on for some sort of course in 'Avila', the Carmelite Monastery some ten or twelve miles away. His information was that this course was titled the 'Life in the Spirit Seminars'.

The parish priest, Fr Tim, quickly reviewed his life in the context of this new development in his parish. He had spent seven years studying in Maynooth before ordination and the 'Life in the Spirit Seminars' formed no part of the curriculum during his years of study there. But now these Johnny-come-lately Charismatics were excitedly telling their friends in his parish that after completion of this course, many of them would be speaking in tongues and more of them would be into things like prophecy, discernment and of all things – healing! Despite his heavy work load, he would, he concluded, just have to make contact with this crowd, to find out what was going on in 'Avila'.

Fr Tim did not become a parish priest from being inactive. So very quickly he called on a lady who was involved in this prayer group affair and she cordially welcomed him. He came to the point without wasting too much time, telling her he was interested in hearing of the 'Life of the Spirit Seminars' in which she was shortly to become involved. In answer to his query, the lady, much to his surprise, opened her Scripture which was on her sitting room table, removed a leaflet from it and handed it to him. Apparently she had gleaned as much information as possible from the authorities in 'Avila' concerning the format and contents of this course, had typed some details on a sheet of paper and had it available for any of the interested prayer group members. There Fr Tim read the programme of events which was to begin in a week's time and which was to continue once a week for seven weeks. Glancing through the typed sheet, he quickly resisted the temptation to point out to her that he thought she would have more than enough to occupy her time, with a husband, a house and three children, rather than signing on for seminars. But, he reflected, the words of the Lord that man (or woman in this case) did not live by bread alone were as valid in that sitting room that morning at that moment as they were two thousand years ago. His host indicated that he was welcome to retain the list of the details of the seminar. Fr Tim thanked her, promised to keep in contact and left.

Before retiring that night Fr Tim studied the typed list to determine the best and easiest way of making contact with this Charismatic group. He hadn't long to wait as at that moment the telephone rang. It was the same lady on the line! Since his visit to her that morning, some people in the prayer group had come together and had discussed their position relative to their parish priest. They had, she informed him, then contacted the authorities in 'Avila' and as a result now wished to invite Fr Tim to concelebrate at the Eucharist on the fifth week of the seminar, when upwards of twenty of his parishioners would be present. Without even consulting his diary he accepted the invitation gladly. Fr Tim realised that surprising things had happened that day. He was surprised at finding a Scripture on her table, surprised at the level of her interest in typing details of the course in question, and surprised how quickly she reacted after his visit, in gathering her group and contacting 'Avila'. He was also surprised at the directness and swiftness of the invitation to 'come and Break Bread with us'. What Fr Tim did not know was that a further surprise was in store for him.

Six weeks after Fr Tim's call to his parishioner, he found himself in 'Avila'. Being one of the 'Life in the Spirit Seminars' team, I was assigned to meet Fr Tim, welcome him and assist him in any way if necessary. Fr Tim was a concelebrant with a Carmelite priest at the Mass for the seminar participants. At this fifth weekly session the members of the seminar team were to lay hands on the participants during the Mass, seeking the release of the gifts of the Holy Spirit in their lives, which gifts they had already received in the Sacraments of Baptism and Confirmation. This event was to take place immediately after the reading of the Gospel. Before it was read the whole assembly praised the Lord in words, then by praying and singing in tongues. There was Fr Tim sitting at the altar with his fellow concelebrant, experiencing for the first time this strange sound.

When the Gospel was read, I approached Fr Tim and invited him to join with another member of the team and myself in laying hands on those assembled. He readily accepted. 'Have you the gift of tongues, Father?' I asked.

'I'm afraid I haven't, Andy,' he replied.

So I informed him that some of those on whom we were to lay hands would receive that gift. He made no comment. The three of us then approached the nearest participant, a man, and laid our hands on him. Immediately we did so, astonishingly, Fr Tim was, as they say, released in tongues. In some amazement my companion and I looked at him, but there he was, with his eyes closed, his hands resting on a kneeling man, while he continued to speak and pray in a new tongue, so spontaneously and naturally. The sounds of this new language flowed effortlessly from him. Going to each one of the participants with us, Fr Tim wished to pray in no other way than in tongues. He was truly enjoying himself! When our task was completed we escorted him back to the altar and there he put his arms around us and in a very calm and steady voice said, 'The Holy Spirit certainly has many surprises for us.' We left him and Mass continued.

At the conclusion of the Breaking of the Break, Fr Tim was surrounded by some two dozen of his parishioners, all members of the new prayer group in his parish and it was a wonderfully joyful gathering. Their prayer group had, I reflected, certainly got off to an auspicious start with the parish priest and his people excitedly discussing the wonder of the manifestation of the release of the gifts of the Holy Spirit which they had just experienced.*

* This event happened in 1981. There are now two prayer groups flourishing in Fr Tim's parish.

9

Strange Souvenirs

It was a cold early January morning as Barbara walked to work. She came to traffic lights and waited there alone. Then with the red lights showing to oncoming traffic, the green man sign duly appeared and Barbara stepped from the footpath on to the road to cross in safety. But one oncoming driver failed, for some unknown reason, to obey the red light sign and continued to drive straight through, his car aimed directly at Barbara. To avoid being hit Barbara stepped back quickly, the car just missing her by a fraction of an inch as the driver continued on his way without, apparently, even noticing the red lights – or Barbara. But in her haste to retreat out of the path of the car, Barbara moving swiftly backwards, hit her left heel against the kerb and fell heavily on her back on to the footpath. She lay there, shocked and badly shaken. But when she attempted to get up, she found to her dismay that she could not do so. Some passers-by rushed to her aid but when they touched her, she cried out in pain, so much so that they realised it would be unwise to endeavour to move her. An ambulance was summoned by telephone from a nearby shop and a flat dweller whose residence overlooked the traffic lights, rushed out and put a rug over the injured girl. Strangely nobody in the vicinity noticed the registration number of the car which was driven so recklessly through the traffic lights nor, unfortunately, could anybody even remember the colour or the make of it. An ambulance with siren wailing, quickly arrived, Barbara was lifted professionally onto the stretcher by the paramedics and whisked away to a Dublin city hospital. Within moments the little knot of bystanders vanished and the street scene returned to normal as if the accident never happened.

In the Casualty centre Barbara gave her name and address and requested that her parents be contacted. The speed of the entire occurrence astonished her. Lying there, she remembered the whole accident in sequence – standing alone at the traffic lights, beginning to walk across the road when the green man showed, hastily backing away from the onrushing car and lastly the fall which had left her now unable to move. There she was in a hospital casualty centre, all in the twinkling of an eye, it seemed. A doctor began gently examining her, while requesting Barbara to tell how the accident happened. She began her story but her words seemed to fade away and she passed out. However, when she regained consciousness she quickly remembered everything which happened, but found herself clad in a strange nightdress and in bed in a hospital ward surrounded by doctors and nurses. At a doctor's request, Barbara found that she could speak, move her head, shoulders, arms, hands, legs and feet. But the whole area of her back was so frightfully painful that she was almost afraid to even breathe. Any attempt to turn on either side brought excruciating pain and as it was impossible for her to stand or walk she had to lie prone. The medical team eventually left, and her distressed parents arrived and Barbara's long hospitalisation had begun, with the days stretching into weeks and eventually into months. But sadly she was making no progress as after exhaustive tests and x-rays, the whole process of physiotherapy, manipulation and traction over a period of six months still left Barbara in a wheel chair, totally unable to stand up or walk.

Jane, married with a teenaged family, regularly attended the 'Avila' prayer meeting, where she constantly heard healing stories. She was also a neighbour and friend of Barbara, was very upset at seeing her in a wheel-chair at twenty years of age and shared the distress of her family. So one evening Jane asked me to call to the hospital and pray with Barbara. She also described the accident and the poor girl's condition. I replied, 'Right – I'll see where the Lord leads me in the matter.' Jane could not comprehend this remark and left the meeting, wondering. However, refusing to be discouraged she rang me at home a few days later and again asked me to visit Barbara. This time I was more forthcoming, and said, 'You know, Barbara may not be interested, possibly her doctors may not approve of it and again Barbara's parents and boy friend might not be happy with the idea.' But Jane stuck to her task and asked, 'Would you like Barbara's mother to contact you and confirm that the family has no objection to your visit?'

'Frankly, I would,' I replied.

So Jane concluded her call by saying, 'Thanks, Andy, her mother will be in touch with you.'

The following night Barbara's mother rang (and I immediately realised that Jane did not put things on the long finger) and confirmed that the whole family would deeply appreciate a visit by me to their daughter. Further, she disclosed that Barbara was to spend the next weekend at home. Hearing this I reacted quickly and said, 'Should your daughter be interested in healing in the name of the Lord maybe she would ring me when she is home at the weekend.' Barbara's mother agreed to arrange this call and then I asked her, 'Would you care to praise the Lord with me now on the telephone to begin the healing in Barbara?' But this suggestion puzzled my caller who asked, 'How can that be done?'

'Should you wish you could repeat the words, "Praise God, Praise the Lord", while I pray spontaneously!' I answered. She gladly agreed so the praising of God began on the telephone and continued for some two or three minutes. Our conversation ended when I said, 'Thanks for ringing and I will be looking forward to Barbara's call provided she is interested and that her medical authorities have no objection.' Somehow I felt that the Lord might be coming into the situation as I reviewed the matter, remembering how Jane had contacted me twice. Now Barbara's mother had entered the story.

The following Saturday evening, Barbara, home for the weekend but in great pain whenever she attempted to leave her wheel-chair, rang. She thanked me for my interest in her, stated that she would be delighted should I find time to visit her in hospital and assured me that the doctors would not have the slightest objection. So I made her an offer saying, 'Would you like to praise the Lord with me now, for your healing?' Barbara having heard of her mother's telephone call was not surprised at this invitation and immediately accepted, so we praised the Lord for the healing which Barbara needed. I then arranged to visit her on the following Wednesday. When the call ended I reflected how strange it was to be praising the Lord with people whom I had never met.

On Wednesday afternoon I found Barbara, dressed in a green track suit, sitting in a wheel-chair beside her bed in a hospital ward, in the company of her parents. I greeted them and thanked them for having me. We chatted for a while as Barbara described how she was injured and her treatmemt to date. She also disclosed that on the following Monday she was being transferred to another hospital to undergo spinal surgery. I then explained a little of the healing ministry after which, with Barbara's consent, I took her hands in mine and praised the Lord for her healing, while asking her parents to join their hands with us. Next I asked Barbara to read some short passages from Scripture, produced the holy oil with which we each made the sign of the cross, and the prayer session ended with the recitation of the Lord's prayer, the Hail Mary and the Gloria. As I was leaving, Barbara's mother invited me to visit her daughter in hospital the following Monday evening. I said I would be delighted to do so.

Barbara never got to the hospital. After the praising of the Lord on that Wednesday afternoon, the nurses lifted Barbara from her wheel-chair, removed her track suit, assisted her to put on her nightie and carried her into bed.

Barbara had a good night's sleep and when she awoke on the following morning, rolled back the coverings, got out of bed slowly – and walked. Her wheel-chair days were over. Barbara's doctors were immediately informed of the dramatic change in her condition and on that Thursday morning she was thoroughly examined. The doctor leading the medical team, when the examination was completed, just stood there in front of Barbara, scratched his head and commented, 'What did you do to yourself? I just don't know what has happened, Barbara.' Next he added, 'When I have an experience like this in medicine, I walk away from it for a while, to gather my thoughts.' And he did just that, deciding to leave matters as they were and to again have a full examination of the patient on the following day. But on Thursday, Barbara continued to stand, walk and sit although her actions were very stiff.

On Friday the medical team examined Barbara once more and at the conclusion of the full clinical examination, her doctor formally presented Barbara with a large envelope containing six x-ray prints of her injured spine and a small envelope containing instructions to a surgeon in the other hospital concerning the spinal operation which had been contemplated. The doctor explained, 'I have cancelled your visit to the hospital and I am discharging you to your home today. But come back to see us in six weeks from now. Bring home these x-ray prints and the letter to the surgeon. Keep them and some day may you have the pleasure of showing them to your children. And don't forget to tell them that the doctor who was treating you was utterly amazed at your healing which he could neither explain nor understand.' Barbara who was proudly wearing an engagement ring, blushed beautifully as she held her strange souvenirs. She was so overawed by the medical team surrounding her that she had not the confidence to say that a travelling man had visited her on the Wednesday of that momentous week in her life and laid his hands on her in the name of the Lord, seeking her total healing.

Exactly one week after my visit to Barbara in hospital, I called to her home by invitation, while on my way to the prayer meeting. There I met Barbara – walking. She was a little stiff but how glad she was to be out of that wheel-chair. On the sitting room table, Barbara proudly displayed the x-ray prints of her spine and the still sealed envelope addressed to the surgeon, happily all now souvenirs. During my visit she disclosed that on the Saturday evening when we prayed on the telephone, after completing arrangements for my visit to the hospital, she experienced some kind of sensation. She couldn't explain it, understand it nor did she expect it. Neither did she mention it to anybody at the time. But whatever happened then was, she asserted, the beginning of her healing.*

As I looked at Barbara I reflected that one week previously when I met her for the first time, she was in a wheel-chair. But there she was now, standing and walking. I was again reminded of Harold Wilson's remark that 'a week is a long time in politics'. Surely a week is a long time in the healing ministry too!

* This incident happened in the Spring of 1984. Barbara walked into 'Avila' to her first prayer meeting in June 1984. At the end of the meeting I introduced her. She received a wonderful welcome.

10

A New Beginning

Eight years have now gone by since my sister's visit to our home to attend a National Conference of the Charismatic Renewal Movement at the Royal Dublin Society, Dublin. When I picked her up that Friday night at the conclusion of the first session of that Conference she was already very involved in the Renewal while I was completely ignorant of it. Nor had I ever heard of such a thing as healing ministry. Events for me have certainly moved rapidly and dramatically since that first encounter and taking a quick look back I am delighted that it all happened. Many times at a prayer meeting and when witnessing instant healings, I thank the Lord for being called to the Renewal, realising that all these exciting events could have been happening all around me and but for the grace of God I would have missed these astonishing experiences.

The reasons why so many healings surface so regularly and constantly in the Charismatic Renewal Movement is an intriguing study which has attracted the attention of theologians, philosophers and psychologists, world-wide. Such serious study will become even more urgent and necessary by people exercising these disciplines as these healings continue to multiply.

The Charismatic Renewal Movement, as it has been known for the past fourteen years or so, is not something completely new. Renewals and reforms of every kind have been experienced by the Church all down the centuries as confirmed by the present Pope when preaching in a Protestant Church in Rome, 'The Church always needs to be reformed.' It will always need renewal too. It is indeed very consoling to realise (especially since Pope John XXIII spread wide his hands and termed the laity the 'People of God') that ordinary guys earning their living in the business world are part and parcel of that Church.

It is widely held that the healings, signs and wonders as

experienced in the Charistmatic Renewal Movement the world over confirm that we, in this our time, have witnessed the greatest outpouring of the gifts of the Holy Spirit since the first Pentecost. Maybe too the people in the Renewal are, by their own life style, possibly writing Acts twenty-nine! and I am certain that it is in the spirit of such assertions that Cardinal Suenens advocates that those involved in the Renewal should read and re-read the Acts of the Apostles. Why, the first Pentecost would have been almost unrecognisable but for its signs and wonders! Surely the power of the Holy Spirit as evidenced by healings must be a sign of contradiction to the atheist, the agnostic, the rationalist, the humanist and to the indifferent in the world of today.

What does the future hold for the Charismatic Renewal Movement? I don't know. But I do know that for the last eight years I have carried in my heart the words of Fr Frank Maher – 'Andy, this is only the beginning – only the very beginning!' There is no way in which I am going to let go of these words of hope.

That such an incredible thing happened to me on a Tuesday night so long ago, is something for which I will be forever grateful.

PRAISE THE LORD!

Prayer Without Frills
Juan Arias

Prayer Without Frills is meant to be a cry of rage and a cry of joy – at one and the same time.

It is *prayer* because it expresses, in words, man's deepest needs and feelings.

It is *without frills* because it does not follow any set patterns, conventions or cultural or religious prejudices. It is simply the real words of every human being who, face to face with the reality of his existence, cries out without fear, without shame and with all the power of his inalienable freedom, everything that he feels is in contradiction to what others impose on him.

It is the prayer of the man who discovers that praying does not mean that he consents to being enslaved *by* anyone or *for* any reason.

It is the prayer of the man who discovers that his God has given him the right to pray, not to beg as an alms but to demand that happiness which God, in a mystery of love, promised him freely, asking only that he accept it.

These prayers spring from the experiences of actual men and women; and they express what many other people are saying as they walk the roads of life, crying aloud to their God and their conscience, searching for solace and newness.

This Tremendous Lover
Eugene Boylan

For thirty years Catholic Christians have been turning and returning to this remarkable spiritual classic in which a Trappist monk speaks clearly and perceptively to the world of priest, religious or layperson still 'in the world'.

It has been called a modern *Introduction to the Devout Life*.

It is a book that takes the question of personal sanctity and relates it to a Pauline vision of the Church as the Mystical Body of Christ.

It is a spiritual reading experience that is very old, ever new, a book which, when read again, remains remarkably fresh and inspiring.

The God I Don't Believe In

Juan Arias

The modern world, it is clear, has gradually developed a completely different approach to God and the Supernatural. We no longer think of Divine Providence riding the clouds in the distant heavens, but as a Father understandable in human terms: warm, accessible, non-authoritarian – a God for all men who have grown weary of the ancient image of an implacable Jehovah.

This 'new' and 'credible' God is the subject of this book – a book which will make, in its warmth and feeling, immediate contact with the reader.

'A real joy; something superb. One must only read it; and then let his heart speak' – *Fruili* (Italian).

Already in Italian, French, German, Portuguese – and now in English, *The God I Don't Believe In* is addressed – with gusto – to all contemporary Christians.

Give Christ Back to Us!

Juan Arias

Here is a challenge to the believer and atheist alike. To the atheist through the sheer breadth of its charity; to the believer through the ruthless sincerity with which it calls on the Christian to face the Godhead implicit in the poorest and least attractive of human beings.

This is a book about man rediscovering God, but for its author God can only be found through, and in the image of, man. Deeper in sympathy and wider in appreciation than most books of theology, this is the work of a priest who has been as it were in the front line of the struggle of faith: for the past fourteen years he has ministered among people who do not believe in God. Perhaps this is what gives his writing such a sharp impact on the reader; why it startles us by the new-minted clarity of its judgments.

The Pursuit of Meaning

Joseph Fabry

The Pursuit of Meaning is written for the millions of people who are healthy but believe they are sick, because they feel empty; for those who are looking for meaning in frantic activity, in money, power, speed, excitement, sex, alcohol, and drugs, or in the pursuit of happiness for happiness' sake; for those who are looking for meaning in laws and rules and dogmas rather than searching for it personally. Every mature person has been expelled from his own paradise and lived through his own concentration camp. To help man endure this has always been the task of prophets, priests, philosophers and educators. Now they are joined by psychologists. Logotherapy supplies one contemporary answer to man's age-old problem of how to live after the expulsion and how to find meaning during and after the trials of sufferings.

Dr Viktor Frankl is the leading figure in what has come to be called the Third Viennese School of Psychotherapy. His writings represent the most important contributions in the field of psychotherapy since the days of Freud, Adler and Jung. He is the author of nineteen books, and his work has been translated into fourteen languages including Japanese and Chinese. His book *Man's Search for Meaning* has sold over a million copies and recently his work *The Doctor and the Soul* was published by Penguin books.

The Pursuit of Meaning is a guide to the theory and application of Viktor E. Frankl's logotherapy and is a very readable book which will appeal to anyone interested in the purpose of life. It is an excellently and clearly written, authoritative and comprehensive presentation of Frankl's system, probably more complete than can be found in any one volume by Frankl himself. It was first published in English in the USA and is now in its third edition. It has been translated and published in Italian, German, Spanish and Japanese.